HUMOLOGY

HOW TO PUT HUMANS BACK AT THE HEART OF TECHNOLOGY

JOANNE GRIFFIN
AND DECLAN FOSTER

R^ethink

First published in Great Britain in 2022 by Rethink Press (www.rethinkpress.com)

Contents

List Of Figures   ix

Preface   1

Terminology – Words Matter   5

PART ONE The Shifting Landscape   7

1. From Homosapiens To Fomosapiens   9

    The Information Age   12

    The dot-com bubble   14

    The platform economy   16

    The spiderweb of things   17

2. Shifting Market Dynamics   19

    Tectonic shifts   20

    For the foreseeable future, the future is unforeseeable   26

3. Man v Machine: A Symbiotic Evolution   31

    Nature or nurture?   32

    The medium is the message   33

The productivity paradox   35

The capacity challenge   37

PART TWO Managing Change   **41**

4. Change Is Hard   **43**

Traditional change management   44

Modern change management   46

Toolkit   48

5. Project Management   **53**

Expertise   54

History   55

Modern approaches   57

Toolkit   59

Behavioural science   62

6. How Disruptive Is Your Product?   **63**

The Change Formula   64

Questions to ask   66

7. Know Your Stakeholders   **69**

Approach   71

Stakeholder matrix   72

8. Practice Makes Perfect   **75**

70:20:10 learning model   77

Measurement   79

9. The SCARF Model   **83**

Status   85

Certainty   86
Autonomy   86
Relatedness   87
Fairness   87

PART THREE Designing With Humans In Mind   **91**

10. The Gatekeepers To The Brain   **93**

Attention and working memory:
The brain's gatekeepers   94
Designing for cognitive load   98
Interaction cost   101

11. Consciously Unconscious   **103**

Dual drivers   105
Familiarity breeds trust   105
The role of habit   109

12. Goldilocks And The Four-Letter Word   **113**

The Goldilocks principle   114
The four-letter word   116

13. Psychological Approaches To Change   **121**

Behavioural approach   122
Cognitive approach   123
Psychodynamic approach   124
Humanistic approach   126

14. Behavioural Design   **129**

What is behavioural science?   130
Behavioural economics   130

Where is behavioural science used today? 131

Behavioural design 134

PART FOUR Seeing Humans Through Five 'I's **139**

15. Impatient **141**

A bird in the hand 143

The billion-dollar pleasure principle 144

The trouble with mindlessness 146

Raising the horizon 148

16. Impressionable **151**

The mechanics of influence 152

The butterfly effect 156

Rise of community – from me to we 157

17. Inattentive **161**

The attention budget 163

The cost of inattention 165

The attention economists 167

Abundance – the enemy of attention 168

18. Inert **171**

Playing for a draw 172

Momentum forces (fuel) 174

Resisting forces (friction) 177

19. Irrational **181**

Irrational reactions 182

Irrational truths 183

Irrational spending 185

Irrational expectations 187

PART FIVE Ethical Design **191**

20. Have You Been Nudged? **193**

Working with humans 194

When is a nudge not a nudge? 195

Types of nudges 197

A framework for ethical nudging 202

21. The Hunter Becomes The Hunted **205**

Unintended consequences 208

Seeing around corners 209

22. The Dark Side Of Influence **213**

The algorithm of you 214

Weapons of mass manipulation 216

Weapons of mass disinformation 218

23. From Egosystems To Ecosystems **223**

Ethics above metrics 225

Do no harm 226

Mercenary or missionary? 229

PART SIX The Humology Approach **233**

24. Know Your Purpose **235**

The Golden Circle 237

Being authentic 239

Attracting talent 240

Purpose statement 241

25. **What Problem Are You Trying To Solve?** 245

The JTBD framework 247

Growth strategy 251

26. **Humology** 253

Know your purpose – why do you
do what you do? 255

Understand the problem 256

Prioritise the human experience – target
behaviours 258

Prioritise the human experience – mapping
existing behaviours 260

Design with intent 262

Deliver the change 264

Reflect and refine 265

Call To Action 269

References 271

The Authors 281

List Of Figures

Figure 1: The widening capacity gap   39

Figure 2: Project constraints   58

Figure 3: Stakeholder matrix   73

Figure 4: 70:20:10 training   78

Figure 5: The bottleneck of working memory   96

Figure 6: Cognitive ease versus cognitive strain   106

Figure 7: The link between user confidence and taking action   108

Figure 8: The science of how habits work   110

Figure 9: Goldilocks spectrum   116

Figure 10: Maslow's hierarchy of needs   127

Figure 11: Behavioural science   133

Figure 12: Clubhouse invitation via text message   158

Figure 13: The cost of multitasking   166

Figure 14: Ethical nudge framework   203

Figure 15: JTBD growth strategies   252

Figure 16: The Humology framework   267

Preface

We are so pleased to welcome you on this journey through *Humology*. This has been a labour of love for us over the past eighteen months. From our bios, you'll see that we each have a differing mix of experience and skillsets, yet we are united in our belief that technology should be designed to work in harmony with human psychology and aspirations.

First and foremost, we hope you enjoy reading this book and find it informative. Secondly, we hope you can apply the learnings in this book and our framework in your professional lives. How you do that will depend on many factors, including your role. A technology founder might use the framework to inform a product's features or design, change how a product is implemented or influence how you communicate about your product. An individual in a corporate transformation role might leverage the framework to increase adoption, reduce overwhelm and lower the risk of change fatigue across an organisation.

The rate of technological evolution we are living through has never been this fast, yet equally will never be this slow again. Technology propagates exponentially while humans evolve in a linear manner. Herein lies the challenge: the disconnection creates a widening gap, and we are already feeling the strain of keeping up. Our brains are overwhelmed with information and we feel a loss of control over technology as a society.

The Internet and social media technologies have enabled us to connect on a global scale like never before and opened our minds to new ideas, locations and cultures that we may never have witnessed without such accessibility. However, the downsides have also been significant. We have crafted industries that depend on human vulnerability and predictability to ensure we remain online, providing lucrative behavioural data to Big Tech.

We shouldn't lose sight of the incredible potential that technology can offer us. Indeed, emerging technologies have the potential to help us solve the existential crises that we face as a species, including climate change, biodiversity and food security.

Humology takes us on a journey through the evolution of technology, its impact on market dynamics and how it is shaping human behaviours. We will look at the complexity of change and the various approaches taken to increase success, including change and project management. We also endeavour to understand human psychology through our Five 'I's framework – Impatient, Impressionable, Inattentive, Inert, Irrational – building knowledge of and respect for human fallibilities.

Of course, no modern discussion of technology would be complete without considering the role of ethical intention in the design of technology. The final section of the book acts as a guide to becoming a humologist. The Humology Approach guides you through the role of purpose, taking a human-first approach to solving challenges with technology, and arms you with the information to make conscious decisions about when to change product design and when to change human behaviours to optimise the value you deliver.

You will find plenty of additional material on our website (www.humology.com), including worksheets, case studies and key takeaways.

We wish you the best of luck on your technology journey.

Declan and Joanne

Terminology – Words Matter

Technologist

This book is for technologists – if you are interested in the role technology plays in our lives, we consider you to be a technologist. If you are designing technology, implementing technology or a consumer of technology, we consider you to be a technologist. Occasionally, we add emphasis to a particular role within our broad definition of technologist – such as a product designer, founder, UX designer or project manager, to illustrate a point.

Users

Users are the humans for whom a product or service is designed. We use this term to represent our role as consumers of technology. It is not intended to discombobulate the human from the user. Our focus is on real, thinking, feeling people – sometime users, always human.

Many of us are technologists and users concurrently. We are all human.

PART ONE
The Shifting Landscape

1
From Homosapiens To Fomosapiens

'The spread of civilisation may be likened to a fire; first, a feeble spark, next a flickering flame, then a mighty blaze, ever increasing in speed and power.'
—Nikola Tesla, inventor of the Tesla coil used in radio technology (Tesla, 1910)

For all but the past 10,000 years, humans have lived in small communities, depending on our skills in gathering food, hunting, fishing and avoiding predators. In the hunt for basic food and shelter, we sought to harness the forces of nature: we carved tools and weapons from stone, tamed wild animals and mastered fire and water. Our human spirit has pursued progress from the beginning of time. From tombs and pyramids, bridges and boats to cars and aeroplanes, we show a yearning hunger for advancement – one invention at a time.

Less than 300 years ago, the Industrial Revolution sparked radical changes in the way we live. During a split-second in evolutionary terms, we invented new sources of power, sailed through uncharted waters and opened up the world in ways we never thought possible. The introduction of Morse code, the printing press, the light bulb and the telephone fundamentally rewired societies and fuelled our quest for even greater innovation.

In a single human life span, we reached stratospheric heights – starting with a stuttering 37-metre flight and culminating in a 750,000-kilometre round trip to the moon.[1,2] The speed at which we adopt new technologies has also rocketed. While the telephone took fifty years to reach an audience of 50 million people, TV reached the same size audience in only twenty-two years. The Internet racked up 50 million users in seven years, while *Pokémon Go* took only nineteen days to have the same impact.[3]

In developing countries, populations have leapfrogged earlier technologies, adopting smartphones quicker than any place on earth. Sub-Saharan Africa has been at the forefront of mobile money adoption

---

1   The Wright brothers' first aeroplane flight on 17 December 1903 lasted just 12 seconds travelling 37 metres over Kitty Hawk, North Carolina.

2   Apollo 11 landed on the moon in July 1969 travelling 384,000 kilometres in 102 hours 45 minutes.

3   J Desjardins, 'How long does it take to hit 50 million users', Visualcapitalist.com, June 8 2018, available at www.visualcapitalist.com/how-long-does-it-take-to-hit-50-million-users

for over a decade, followed closely by East Asia and Pacific regions. Digital banking has revolutionised financial inclusion in these previously underserved populations, offering access to new markets and services.

This is how technology enters and reshapes societies: bit by bit, at first – until we can't imagine life without it. Once a critical mass of acceptance is reached, attention shifts to the next target. Buoyed by the inventions of our past, we dream up a new future and set about making it our reality. It's breathtaking to take stock of the degree to which we have evolved the world around us.

Technology years seem to act like dog years – for every trip we take around the sun, technology appears to advance at a much faster rate. Moore's Law (the power of computing will double every 18 to 24 months), its relation Koomey's Law (the amount of battery needed for a fixed computing load will fall by a factor of two every 18 months) and Kryder's Law (the amount of data storable in a given space will double every two years) mean that technology becomes more powerful and more affordable every year. Whether we consider the advancements exponential or not, the reality is that technology is advancing at a faster rate than society can consume it, or keep pace with it. When technological evolution continues to outpace human evolution, the result is 'human lag'. We experience lag when we feel overwhelmed and unable to keep up with the impact emerging technologies has on our lives. Throughout this book, we will touch on the many underlying causes of human lag, including resistance to change, learning anxiety, biases and inertia.

The Information Age

In March 1989, Tim Berners-Lee wrote a proposal while at CERN outlining his ideas for the Web as a global hypertext information-sharing space.[4] Within a couple of months of receiving internal approval, Berners-Lee had published the world's first web browser and web server. In 1991, he invited collaborators to join his 'WorldWideWeb' project via a public newsgroup, kicking off a wave of euphoria throughout the tech industry. And just like that, we entered the Information Age.

Over the next ten years, the Internet went mainstream, enabling one-to-many communications in a way we had never seen before. In 1994, a young Jeff Bezos left a lucrative senior vice president role at a Wall Street hedge fund to register the domain name 'Amazon. com'. Bezos believed there was an opportunity to act as an intermediary between buyers and sellers on the Internet. While the concept of monetising the position of the middleman was hardly innovative, Bezos had a hunch that the Internet would enable him to reach

---

4   CERN refers to the European Organization for Nuclear Research.

customers in a way that bricks-and-mortar businesses simply could not.

By the late 1990s, Microsoft, Amazon, eBay and Yahoo emerged as the darlings of the Internet. These were the heady days of the dot-com boom.[5] Venture capital flowed freely, tech valuations rocketed, and investors swapped out traditional stocks in favour of the latest tech IPO.[6] Meanwhile, Sergey Brin and Larry Page dropped out of Stanford to work on a project called 'Google' and teenage Bostonian Shawn Fanning launched Napster, the world's first peer-to-peer file-sharing software for audio files.

Napster delighted consumers and enraged industry bigwigs. Despite sustaining buoyant CD sales, the music industry suffered financially, prompting a furious slew of lawsuits that ultimately led to Napster shutting down in 2001. While the music industry celebrated its victory, consumers had tasted the forbidden fruit and a flurry of file-sharing sites proliferated long after Napster was silenced. If Amazon primed us with a frictionless buying experience and endless choice, Napster introduced us to the lure of instant gratification.

---

5 A dot-com is a company with an online business model. Dot-coms get their name from the .com at the end of their website URLs
6 An initial public offering (IPO) is when a company raises cash by issuing shares that are publicly listed on one or more stock exchanges. Otherwise known as 'going public'.

While the music industry poured millions into defending its copyright against online piracy, Steve Jobs spotted an opportunity to capture the music streaming market and keep the pockets of powerful music moguls well-lined. In October 2001, Apple introduced the iPod with iTunes following soon after. While it wasn't the first MP3 player to come to market, Apple's user-friendly design was a big hit with customers, propelling the company to explosive growth over the next decade. The iPod not only revolutionised the music industry, it laid the groundwork for portable technologies – proving that a 'computer in your pocket' had an enthusiastic tribe longing for something they didn't yet know they needed.

This was the era of consumer-friendly innovation during which the raw impact of technological disruption was borne by patriarchy and traditional billion-dollar industries. In the years that followed, consumers raced to embrace the latest technological innovation leaving many valuable businesses licking their wounds, unable to comprehend or compete in this new digital world.

The dot-com bubble

During the late 1990s, we bore witness to the frenzied race for tech start-ups to go public. From our vantage point in large global consulting firms, we watched as average Joes became paper millionaires overnight. It wasn't unusual for these companies to double their valuation on their first day of trading, making a tidy profit for their early investors. Many dot-coms during this era bought into the 'get big fast' (GBF) strategy characterised by low pricing, a heavy marketing spend and strategic alliances that created barriers to entry for competitors. In the race for market dominance, success was measured in user numbers rather than financial terms.

However, by April 2000, only one month after reaching a historic peak, the NASDAQ shed 34% of its value (Simply Wall St, 2014). Trillions of dollars in wealth vanished overnight. The following year, the shock events of 9/11 reverberated through the global economy, drying up the cash that fuelled the creativity and experimentation of the dot-com era.

While many industry commentators enjoyed some indulgent *Schadenfreude* – denouncing the Internet as a fad – many of the businesses that survived this period are among the world's most valuable companies in history. As Silicon Valley was licking its wounds, a new generation of tech-savvy students was dreaming up the next iteration of the Internet – Web 2.0. If a one-to-many business model defined the first iteration of the Web, Web 2.0 ushered in an era of democratisation and participation. Social networking, social media, blogging and photo and video sharing – whatever we wanted to share, there was an app for it.

The platform economy

By the early 2000s, encouraged by the early successes of Friendster and Myspace, the new darlings of the social age started to emerge.[7,8] First LinkedIn and then Facebook invited users to sign up to their platforms to connect with each other. Finding the offer of free services and feeling closer to God-like celebrities too tempting to rebuff, we joined in our millions. In contrast with dot-com companies who spent heavily on advertising to stimulate growth, Web 2.0 companies fuelled rapid global growth by leveraging two key concepts: built-in sharing capabilities and network effects. Unlike traditional businesses that control the means of production, these emerging business models controlled the means of *connection*. Some of the largest platforms in the world now own the infrastructure on which other platforms are built, for example, Apple and iOS, Google and Android, Amazon and AWS, Microsoft and Azure, and Meta and React Native.

This was also the era of 'me' – a time when we explored our individuality online, defined by the meteoric rise to fame of people we had never heard

---

7 Friendster was 'an online community that connects people through networks of friends for dating or making new friends' according to its landing page when it launched in 2002. While the user base grew to over ten million, a series of site performance issues caused users to abandon the platform in droves.

8 Myspace was a social media network platform that allowed users to engage in forums, listen to music and create their own profile page. From 2005 to early 2009, it was the largest social networking site in the world, eventually giving way to Facebook.

of. By the late 2000s, society was being rewired for the digital age. Smartphones came with embedded cameras to facilitate our need to capture every moment for our followers. Social media platforms raised our FOMO (fear of missing out) levels to new heights. The perception that other people are leading more interesting lives, having more fun and being more successful became strangely addictive to us. FOMO acts like a self-perpetuating cycle – the more FOMO we experience, the more helpless we feel and the more we engage with social media.

The spiderweb of things

Intersecting trends have historically produced the biggest tectonic shifts. There was a time when hopping into a stranger's car or sleeping at a stranger's house would seem implausible. However, in a noisy world with too much information and infinite choice, a new recipe for success emerged. Pick a market, curate its content, mix in some social proof and top it off with frictionless convenience – hey presto, you have the makings of Uber, DoorDash, Twitter, Pinterest, Airbnb and many more.

The evolution of no-code applications will continue to broaden the reach of technology. Spurred by an initial shortage of skilled software developers, these visual drag-and-drop interfaces are rewiring how software is built – and who builds it. Not only can we build faster and more cheaply, using fewer resources than ever before, we no longer need a degree in engineering, usability or design. The rise of the citizen developer will enable more of us to bring our ideas to life faster than we ever have before. We are no longer living at the speed of humanity; we are marching to the beat of rapid technological evolution.

What socio-technological challenges lie ahead? In what ways can we continue these incredible innovations while safeguarding our collective humanity? No single company acting alone can unlock real opportunity or excel in a hyperconnected future. The enormous power of artificial intelligence (AI) systems can no longer be regulated on a national level. Global consequences call for global action.

We have written this book because, to paraphrase Maya Angelou, when we know better, we do better (Angelou, 2018). How can researchers, designers, engineers and policymakers engage in the design and development of tools and technology to support human flourishing in all its richness – to enable human beings to grow and develop, to manifest what they value and to act meaningfully and ethically in the world?

2
Shifting Market Dynamics

'I'd put my money on the sun and solar energy. What a source of power! I hope we don't have to wait until oil and coal run out before we tackle that.'
— Thomas Edison, inventor (Newton, 1987)

Now and again, entire ecosystems experience a step-change powered by a collision of independent exponential technologies. For many constituents of an ecosystem, this step-change can feel like mental whiplash. We use the term 'mental whiplash' to describe the sudden jolt we experience when disruptive change displaces current norms and forces us to speed up or take a rapid step forward. We can experience this individually, as an industry or as an ecosystem. The initial response is one of dizzying confusion followed by a period of languishing and taking stock. We believe that the technology industry is experiencing such a moment right now.

Technology is neither inherently good nor evil. It can, however, magnify the risk and impact of unethical decisions. While human creativity and genius are responsible for many of our greatest achievements, these same capabilities have led to many of the challenges we've created for ourselves today. Socioeconomic inequity, surveillance capitalism, market shocks and a myriad of other industrial, environmental and social challenges serve as stark reminders of our myopic optimism. We have yet to create equally sophisticated solutions in response.

That these are challenges created by humans means that we must take a long-term view and a human approach to crafting solutions. We are in urgent need of a compass to guide the way we create, design and use technology – with renewed purpose, solid ethics and an awareness of risk.

Tectonic shifts

Just as Earth's crustal plates grind violently against each other from time to time, resulting in cataclysmic earthquakes, tsunamis and volcanic eruptions, we are experiencing comparable turmoil as new technologies grind against traditional structures. Governments, regulators, banks, markets and traditional economic models are creaking under the unrelenting pressure of change, with wide-ranging consequences.

Data – the gold rush of the digital age

We are awash with data and it is growing at an unprecedented pace. In 2021, it was estimated that we generated, replicated and consumed 79 zettabytes of data (79 trillion gigabytes), a statistic that is projected to double over the next five years (Holst, 2021). As we conduct our lives online, we leave a trail of digital breadcrumbs behind us – websites we visit, our social media activity, searches we conduct and content we create. These breadcrumbs act like a digital fingerprint that can be analysed to create a psycho-demographic profile, or a human digital twin, used to simulate our interests, decisions and preferences.[9]

With billions of devices exchanging data online every day, existing 4G networks are becoming congested. Fifth-generation (5G) networking promises greater capacity, superfast speeds and real-time connectivity, opening up a world of possibilities in areas where instant response times are most critical, such as autonomous cars, live event broadcasts, remote surgeries and interactive gaming.

---

9   If you're curious about what the Internet knows about you, we encourage you to check out the University of Cambridge's research project Apply Magic Sauce, available at: https://applymagicsauce. com/demo

As data volumes continue to grow, the issues of data sovereignty and privacy are increasingly pervasive. The wide-scale collection and monetisation of online behavioural data are eroding privacy and decaying trust. With personal data considered a valuable asset, data breaches and cybersecurity risks will remain a central focus of technologists.

Global citizenship

A digitally connected world without borders represents endless opportunities for technologists. However, with great power comes great responsibility. The potential to do harm, overlook cultural nuances or exclude large swathes of the population is also heightened. Unleashing technology products into global markets carries additional risks for technologists, leading to a host of unintended consequences.

When legislation emerges in foreign markets, it has global ramifications. Because it's easier for digital platforms to apply a uniform set of rules across their global operations, the strictest rules typically become the baseline. For example, the reach of the EU's General Data Protection Regulation (GDPR) stretches far beyond the borders of its member states, creating waves of change in global markets.[10] The GDPR applies to all businesses that collect or process

---

10   The General Data Protection Regulation came into effect on 25 May 2018 in all member states to harmonise data privacy laws across Europe.

EU citizens' data, regardless of the company's location. Some of the largest fines have been issued by the smallest countries in the world: Luxembourg imposed a fine of $865 million on Amazon, while the Irish Data Protection Commissioner fined WhatsApp €225 million (Tessian, 2022). Following the EU's example, the Brazilian government enacted their General Data Protection Law (LGPD) in 2018, shaping the way companies process the data of Brazilians. Similarly, the California Consumer Privacy Act (CCPA) enacted in 2020 aims to protect the data of residents of the state of California. With further legislation forthcoming in a number of other jurisdictions (India, Nigeria, Kenya, South Africa), technologists will need to keep pace with the global ramifications of domestic legislation.

Buyers and sellers

The traditional lengthy sales process to a C-suite buyer is undergoing its own shift – from a top-down model where the selection process is completed at the C-suite level to a bottom-up model where end-users influence the selection process – altering the way we sell, select and consume technology products and services. This represents a complete rewiring of the internal organisation.

Today's technologists need to accommodate an increasing array of key stakeholders: the buyer-gatekeeper with a long list of requirements, the irrational decision-maker seeking a silver bullet app, the security-conscious chief technology officer (CTO), the distracted and overwhelmed user, the technophobe, the early adopter and everything in between. Successful negotiations now require an understanding of the goals, biases, preferences and attitudes of every one of these roles and an awareness of the culture of the organisation you are selling into.

SaaSy technology

A combination of infrastructure innovation, greater affordability and changing customer behaviour has sparked demand for Software as a Service (SaaS) applications. SaaS apps are an attractive proposition to businesses unwilling to invest capital in a technology infrastructure that is likely to change quickly. Today's users don't want to *own* technology, they don't even want to *use* technology – they just want to get their job done as efficiently as possible and move on.

The implications for technologists are wide-ranging. SaaS business models intensify the market's fixation with user growth and predictable revenue streams. Today's version of the 'get big fast' strategy, which defined the dot-com era, has one distinctive difference – rather than relying on advertising to win new customers, we let the product do the talking. A product-led growth (PLG) strategy often incorporates many of the psychological hacks used by the advertising industry directly into the product itself. Ultimately, the goal is to get users to adopt a product through habitual usage. The deeper the habit, the more sticky the product is.

Many SaaS apps employ a 'try before you buy' strategy – delivering value before asking for payment. This approach allows a wide range of potential users to get a glimpse at the value a product can offer so that they can weigh up the cost of making an investment. Free trials for a limited period of time are ideal for products that solve a pain point within a short timeframe and are intuitive to use. For more complex tasks, freemium models provide limited functionality for free, charging a fee as the user needs additional functionality. However, the explosion of SaaS tools is contributing to SaaS creep, the emergence of 'Shadow IT' teams, and app overload for individuals.

The paradox of choice

We are spoilt for choice – there is an increasing array of apps ready and willing to cater to our every human need. Take the world of fitness: App Annie estimates that a further 71,000 health and fitness apps were released in 2020 (Sydow, 2021). The proliferation of choice poses a challenge for users and developers alike. We easily become overwhelmed by choice. Increasingly, we look to our social groups or people we trust to help curate the myriad of options available to us.

In a bid to stand out from the competition and attract the attention of potential users, tech companies are devising progressively creative tactics. However, with many suffering from 'shiny object syndrome', companies are dealing with a deluge of new users who fail fast and churn quickly. We're a fickle bunch – if we can't extract value easily, we'll search for another tool that gets the job done easier, cheaper and better.

For the foreseeable future, the future is unforeseeable

If the last decade was dominated by the trendy buzzword 'VUCA' (volatility, uncertainty, complexity and ambiguity), 2020 was an inflection point. For the first time since 2004, the Oxford English Dictionary was unable to issue a Word of the Year because there were simply too many words to choose from. The year 2020 brought a whole new vocabulary: Covid-19, quarantini, Black Lives Matter, social distancing, WFH (working from home), doomscrolling and cancel culture. Like us, the English language has had to adapt rapidly.

Futurist Jamais Cascio proposes a new buzzword to represent our present reality – BANI (brittle, anxious, nonlinear and incomprehensible). Social structures like governments, civil service, legislators and banks are creaking under the pressure of change. As Cascio (2020) states, 'Brittle systems do not fail gracefully, they shatter'. In an interconnected world, a ripple can quickly turn into a tsunami.

Enter the behavioural scientists

Long before the data gold rush and AI, marketing campaigns by Coca-Cola, Apple and P&G steadily built tribes of loyal followers – winning hearts and minds through behavioural insights. P&G continues to invest in behavioural science to embed its products habitually into our everyday lives through habit-stacking – tying the everyday process of brushing our teeth (using Crest toothpaste) with our morning gratitude practice, for example (Lee, 2019).

There are now over 200 institutions applying behavioural insights to public policy around the world (OECD, 2020). Leading thinkers in the behavioural sciences have been awarded Nobel Prizes for their work, behavioural science books frequently top bestseller lists, and organisations are tapping behavioural scientists to tackle their people problems. Tech companies such as Google, Amazon, Spotify and Netflix have been at the forefront of applied behavioural science for a long time. Today, even smaller tech companies, such as Headspace, Calm, Noom and Robinhood, employ teams of behavioural scientists to build habits for their users. That such major international organisations are creating dedicated behavioural science teams is a testament to the discipline's power to create real impact.

From black swans to black elephants

When world events feel incomprehensible, we're inclined to refer to them as 'black swans' – unlikely and unexpected events that have vast consequences. These 'unknown unknowns' invoke our most primal fear, the fear of the unknown (FOTU), and shake our sense of stability to the core (Carleton, 2016). In reality, many recent disasters were not 'unknown unknowns' – the risks were identified but not addressed. As in the fantastical disaster movie *Don't Look Up*, when faced with complex challenges that are beyond our control, we engage in denial. Like the proverbial elephant in the room, we conspire to look past it.

So, what do you get when we cross a black swan with the elephant in the room? You guessed it – a black elephant – a substantial and complex problem that is visible to everyone but no one wants to address (Friedman, 2014). Global warming, biodiversity extinction and infectious diseases all represent black elephant events.

Today's business models need to be agile, resilient and capable of identifying, assessing and addressing emerging risks as they arise. AI enables the analysis of huge swathes of data to identify shifts in patterns and predict outcomes, making it possible for us to build risk management into our business models. A hyper-connected world makes it easier than ever to build a diverse network and stay on top of emerging trends. Armed with the right tools, we can avoid a stampede.

From egosystems to ecosystems

According to traditional economics, the purpose of a company is to maximise shareholder value, taking a 'me above you' approach to business. These business models have a myopic focus on maximising shareholder value from quarter to quarter while building moats around their products to protect their dominant market position. The result of this egotistical winner-takes-all model has been the concentration of 44% of the world's wealth among only 1% of its population (Credit Suisse, 2021).

However, change is afoot. Newer businesses, and some established companies, are adopting a 'we above me' approach. Stakeholder capitalism is one such response. Businesses adopting a stakeholder mindset believe in creating value for all stakeholders – customers, employees, partners, communities, the planet and society. However, while the shift is underway in business, markets are lagging behind when it comes to adjusting their expectations of infinite growth in a finite world.

We are also seeing businesses taking a more collaborative approach to creating value – embracing innovation, co-creation, community and platform interoperability. Taking an ecosystem approach not only diversifies risk and builds natural resilience into emerging technologies, it can also be a powerful accelerator. Like the technological ecosystem, the collective value of a healthy business ecosystem is greater than the sum of its parts. If you want to go far, go together.

Among the most difficult questions about any paradigm shift are these: What can you do now while markets are in transition, and how can you prepare for the future? Many technologists lack even a basic framework for connecting directly with the humans who use their products. This means they make decisions based on limited knowledge and react to unexpected events in real time. An urgent need exists for a practical guide, based on proven models, that leaders anywhere in the world can use to ensure that ethical human-first principles are integrated into the design and delivery of technology. This is the call to action for *Humology* – the restoration of balance between humanity and technology. The stakes are high while the entry bar is low.

3
Man v Machine: A Symbiotic Evolution

'It is primarily through the growth of science and technology that man has acquired those attributes which distinguish him from the animals, which have indeed made it possible for him to become human.'
— Arthur Holly Compton, physicist
(Compton, 1940)

As the world becomes increasingly digital, our concentration levels are dwindling. Unable to read a book or stay focused for long periods of time, we trawl the internet searching for a nugget of content to quell our appetite. The rush of pleasure we feel as we hurriedly consume our digital snack is intoxicating enough to keep us coming back for more. In fact, skimming is fast becoming our dominant mode of reading. The more we use the internet, the more the neural circuits devoted to scanning, skimming and multitasking are strengthened, while those that support deep focus are weakened (Carr, 2011). At the same time, the number of adults with ADHD has increased 123% from 2013–2016 (Kent, 2022). Just as snacking on empty calories takes a toll on our physical health, could the nutritional content of our digital 'feed' be impacting our focus and attention?

Nature or nurture?

Throughout our lives, the human brain develops layer by layer, beginning before birth and continuing well into old age. Genes provide the foundation, while experience shapes the brain's architecture. A newborn's brain contains a staggering 100 billion neurons, primed and ready to start forming new neural connections as soon as we open our eyes or hear our first sounds. These neurons continue to learn through experience – the more experience they have, the more effortless that task becomes. Connections between neurons also grow stronger through repetition, hence the saying 'neurons that fire together, wire together'.

Over time, learning and experience physically rewire the brain, forming an intricate network of high-speed information superhighways. To maintain some order in this ever-expanding circuitry, the brain embraces a 'use it or lose it' philosophy, deleting unused neural connections to make way for new ones. This process of neural adaptation, known as neuroplasticity, stays with us throughout our lives and is largely responsible for how we adapt to changes in our environment.

However, while plasticity can be a superpower, it can also be our Kryptonite. Once we have built fast super-highways, we are naturally reluctant to travel slower routes. Our preference for speed can also promote repetitive and rigid patterns of behaviour, according to psychiatrist Norman Doidge (2007). Doidge notes that our brain's plasticity also begins to decline as we enter our mid-twenties. A reduction in plasticity makes it increasingly difficult for us to adapt to change even when we want to. As plasticity declines, we are more likely to seek comfort in the familiar, and become more protective of our own beliefs. Faced with change, a rigid brain will seek to preserve the status quo – fighting to change the external world rather than changing our inner world.

The medium is the message

A mounting body of evidence shows that digital life is physically rewiring our brains. In the 1960s, Canadian educator Marshal McLuhan reasoned that the *way* in which we consume information has more influence than the information itself. He believed that as we moved from passive consumers of static TV schedules to multitasking participants in a 24/7 online global village, we've developed an appetite for speed, convenience and interaction (McLuhan, 1964).

While baby boomers are accustomed to reading books left-to-right, or instructions beginning-to-end, younger people growing up in a noisier world have become super-scanners. Scanning is the brain's ingenious response to information overload – quickly filtering out superfluous content to identify what is worthy of our attention. It's as if our cognition systems are shifting from linear sequential thinking to non-linear parallel processing, to cope with a faster, more complex world.

The way we store information has also changed over the past decade. As we become more reliant on our phones to store contact details or on Facebook to remind us of birthdays, we increasingly depend on our transactive memory – which stores *where* to find information rather than the information itself. Scientists refer to this phenomenon as digital amnesia or the 'Google effect'. We no longer store readily accessible information in our brains because it is so easy to 'Google it' (Sparrow et al, 2011). This evolutionary adaptation protects our brains from information overload by incorporating readily-available external storage solutions. The fact that our brains have adapted to strategically offloading parts of our memory onto digital devices while relying on our ability to find information rather than on our ability to remember it is pretty impressive! Expanding our memory to incorporate a distributed storage network frees up valuable cognitive resources to help us keep pace in a changing world. It does, however, raise concerns about the security and reliability of this novel external storage system.

The productivity paradox

Despite the hype about technology making us more productive, we seem to be working more hours – not less. And while we feel busier than ever, it's hard to avoid the feeling that we're not getting very much done. How can that be? Why is it that in spite of technological advances, we seem to be working harder than ever? Are humans becoming the bottleneck as technology continues its march?

As more and more things compete for our attention, there are still only twenty-four hours in a day and we can only ingest so much information at one time. The robotic revolution promised to emancipate us from repetitive, mundane tasks so that we could be more productive, take on more fulfilling work and work fewer hours. However, in reality, we are working longer hours and more intensely than ever, while measures of productivity merely inch ahead. Making things faster does not in itself guarantee that we become more productive. In our experience, a proliferation of applications that solve narrow-use cases coupled with poorly designed enterprise technologies that require workers to rewire how they work have made it more difficult to keep up and leave us feeling overwhelmed.

An abundance of personal and workplace apps intended to make our lives easier has inadvertently created 'app overload'. This digital fragmentation has a detrimental impact on productivity. A survey of 2,000 knowledge workers found that 69% of workers waste up to an hour a day navigating between apps, with most toggling between apps up to 10 times per hour (RingCentral, 2018)! This constant toggling between browsers, apps, devices and messages impedes our ability to process and retain information, decreases our ability to filter out superfluous information, fragments our focus, and leads to error.

This form of forced multitasking is like grazing all day long without eating a solid meal and wondering why you feel shattered by the end of the day. Constant context switching erodes productivity and leads to cognitive fatigue. When we spread our attention too thin, clutter is left behind as we transition to a new task. Professor Sophie Leroy refers to this clutter as 'attention residue', when part of our attention remains focused on a prior task while we transition to a new one (Leroy, 2009). The impact is reduced attentional focus and psychological presence. Think of your brain like an internet browser with 20+ tabs open at any one time – eventually we need to close out of each tab and clear the cache to prevent the browser from slowing down. Just like an open browser tab consumes resources, our brain finds it hard to ignore an incomplete task, and instead keeps it active in the back of our mind even when we are trying to focus on and perform other tasks.

In 2021, Microsoft's Human Factors Lab investigated the impact of back-to-back meetings on our cognitive abilities with similar findings. Using electroencephalogram (EEG) caps to monitor brain activity, participants engaged in two hours of back-to-back meetings without taking a break. The results are stark. Without adequate time to transition between meetings, attention residue showed increased cortisol levels in the brain, reducing focus and engagement (Microsoft, 2021).

The capacity challenge

While the potential for technology to augment humanity is momentous, humans are drinking from a fire hose to keep up with the pace of change. The speed of our adaptation is hampered by digital fragmentation, attention-hacking and unnecessary disruption introduced by technology. We refer to this widening gap between the pace of evolution of technology and that of humanity as the capacity challenge. As the rate of technological advancement picks up, individuals and organisations are wasting precious cognitive resources filtering out noise, dealing with app overload, and navigating a volatile world. The result is that individuals and organisations lag behind the rapid evolution of technology.

In calmer times, we can rely on our surge capacity to help us through periods of adversity. Surge capacity refers to our emergency reserves – a collection of mental and physical resources we can draw on for short-term survival in acutely stressful situations such as a global pandemic, or a war. We can run on adrenaline for a short period of time, but it's not sustainable in the longer term for our body or mind. In recent years, many of us have depleted our surge capacity without the opportunity to replenish these critical reserves. Operating on low reserves compromises our ability to cope with change in our personal and professional lives. When change fatigue sets in, we feel increased negative reactions, frustration and apathy. Add in app overload and you have a perfect storm of overwhelm.

While rewiring and reorganising a single brain takes effort, rewiring an entire organisation is infinitely more complex. Organisations are built for stability and longevity, not speed and agility. Faced with the quickening pace of creative destruction, today's organisations are under increasing pressure to adapt faster than ever. A recent study by Gartner found that a worker's ability to cope with change is 50% of what it was pre-pandemic. What's especially interesting is that smaller changes created *more* change fatigue than a single large-scale change. Changes that impact a person's day-to-day life, such as moving to a new team or getting a new manager, impact employees 2.5 times *more* than larger, more structural changes (Antliff, 2021). Based on these findings, it follows that smaller changes can have a disproportionate impact on an organisation's productivity.

Technology is taking the lead as we slowly fall behind, running to stand still. Left unaddressed, the gap between humans and technology could quickly become a chasm.

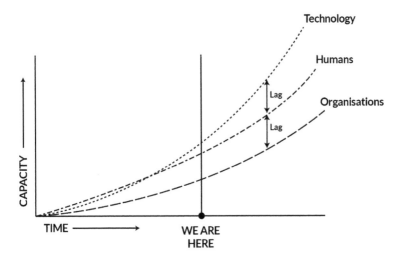

Figure 1 *The widening capacity gap*

As a technologist, you have the power to correct this imbalance.

The critical challenge is whether we can increase the human curve to meet the technology curve. To do so, we must protect the human capacity to adapt and acquire new skills. The design of digital solutions can optimise for learning and information diffusion, while promoting flow and replenishment. Technologists can also help eliminate unnecessary change and disruption by creating digital solutions to human problems in a more thoughtful manner. In a world where technology empowers rather than disrupts humanity – we all win.

Throughout this book, we highlight the role of technologists in bringing humanity and technology closer together. All change starts with awareness.

PART TWO
Managing Change

4
Change Is Hard

'If you want to make enemies, try to change
something.'
    — Woodrow Wilson, 28th US President
    (Moran, 2003)

Change management, sometimes called organisational change management (OCM), is a structured approach to moving an organisation from a current state to a desired future state, focusing on the people side of change. On technology projects, OCM is used to achieve a faster speed of adoption, higher ultimate utilisation and a greater level of overall proficiency in using the new tool. On these projects, the change manager's role is to ensure that the change is accepted, adopted and embedded in the organisation. The scope of the change manager's role will typically focus on change impact assessments, communications and learning. In addition, they may provide sponsor support, line manager coaching, go-live readiness assessment and go-live support.

Why is this relevant for technologists? Today, prominent technology vendors and system integrators use change management to ensure the successful implementation of their products. When pitching for work at more significant clients, you might also find that the change management function is part of the selection process. So, it can help to understand their perspective and terminology. We believe that understanding change management and leveraging the knowledge and toolkits can provide any technologist with a competitive advantage. This gives every implementation of your product a greater chance of success, leading to better customer satisfaction and increased product-led growth. Start-ups have yet to benefit from the value and true potential of these approaches, giving those who embrace change management approaches a clear competitive advantage.

Traditional change management

In the mid to late twentieth century, many researchers and thought leaders from the social sciences, psychology and business began to pull together the strings of the body of knowledge that would become known as change management. As far back as the late 1940s, Lester Coch and John RP French, Jr researched change resistance in a clothing factory (Lawrence, 1969). Kurt Lewin (1947) created a three-stage model, summarised as 'unfreeze-change-freeze', which was later built on by Edgar Schein (1996). This model gave organisations a structured approach for managing change; however, it is probably no longer relevant to today's changes, which seem to happen in overlapping waves.

Other notable contributions came from Elizabeth Kübler-Ross and John Kotter. In her seminal work, *On Death And Dying*, Kübler-Ross outlined the five stages of grief that she noted from her work with cancer patients (Kübler-Ross, 1969). These stages are familiar to most of us now: denial, anger, bargaining, depression and acceptance. People involved in the emerging discipline of change management saw parallels between her work and those undergoing profound changes in organisations. These parallels were taken a bit too literally. Still, they were foundational to later iterations of the change curve such as Adams, Hayes and Hopson's 'change curve' (Cameron & Green, 2015), which is still used by many change management practitioners today in various formats. We prefer Daryl Conner and Robert Patterson's 'change commitment curve', which is more relevant to technology adoption (Conner, 2006). The curve illustrates the various stages of commitment that people go through when they experience any change, which includes new technology. We start at the initial contact stage and go all the way through to the internalisation stage, which is the highest level of commitment you can make to any change (Blaga, 2014).

We like to think of John Kotter as the godfather of modern change management. In his book *Leading Change,* first published in 1996, Kotter introduced us to his 'eight-step process for leading change', which significantly influenced the field (Kotter, 2012). Change management started to appear on management's radar in the 1990s. This is mainly due to the business community recognising the shortcomings of the re-engineering boom of the 1980s, which was primarily focused on business process redesign and workforce reductions, with little or no regard for the people side of change or the impact on organisational culture. In addition, the 1990s saw a massive increase in the number of sizeable multiyear enterprise resource planning (ERP) projects using products such as SAP or Oracle. Organisations and vendors started to realise that there was a need for expertise focusing not only on the technology but the people side of change. The bigger consultancies realised that deploying change resources and teams on these larger projects also opened up additional revenue opportunities.

Modern change management

Today, change management is seen as a leadership and management competency, a body of knowledge and a profession. An increasing number of professionals choose change management as a career, as shown by a simple search of your favourite local job website. Those in the profession come from an interesting mix of backgrounds, including training, management consulting, project management and counselling. Organisations like the Change Management Institute, the Association of Change Management Professionals and Prosci provide accreditation and bodies of knowledge. Nowadays, you can study change management at Master's level. Change management is also typically included in the top five competencies that any aspiring leader needs.

Making the critical distinction between the role of a change manager and that of a project manager can also be helpful. The two roles are often confused or conflated. While there are distinct differences between them, they also have quite a lot in common and can be seen as two sides of the same coin. Change managers and project managers regularly have to work side by side to deliver a project or achieve a successful transformation. Problems can arise when their roles and responsibilities are misunderstood or confused.

A project manager's focus is to ensure that projects are delivered on time, to budget, within the agreed scope and of appropriate quality. A change manager will focus on the people side of change to ensure that the change is accepted, adopted and embedded in the organisation. Project managers tend to have expertise in facts and figures and deal with return on investment (ROI), risks and issues, business cases and project deliverables. Change managers tend to have expertise in perceptions and emotions, ie how impacted stakeholders perceive the change and how it affects them, and how they respond emotionally to the change. We will delve a little deeper into project management in Chapter 5.

As change management practices become more mature in larger organisations, we have seen the advent of the change management office (CMO). These departments increase 'the effectiveness and efficiency of change management by providing commonality and a single go-to point. The group also provides value and creates credibility for the change management capability journey by demonstrating the commitment senior leaders have made in establishing this center' (Prosci, nd).

Toolkit

Having understood the relevance and importance of change management, we can now turn our attention to some of the methods and tools that change managers use to achieve successful and sustainable changes within organisations. We are confident that you can use some or all of these to gain a competitive advantage:

- **Change impact register:** In a change impact register, for each impact, change managers will document the current state, the future state, the delta or difference, and the proposed action or intervention to address the impact. Also, you can consider including a rating and a category for each impact and an owner for each action.

- **Stakeholders:** Identifying, assessing and managing stakeholders are key components of any successful change. Change managers will work with key project personnel to identify all stakeholders, understand their unique needs and interest in the change, and devise an approach to keep them engaged with the process or win them over to the change.

- **Communications and engagement:** The communications and engagement plan is developed to ensure that the right people get the right messages from the right people at the right time. Change managers will ensure a proper mix of electronic communication and face-to-face engagement, and that communication goes two ways, ie the project is actively listening to the feedback received.

- **Learning:** A learning strategy will typically have three components: a training needs analysis (TNA), delivery and measurement, and an evaluation approach. The TNA will determine and articulate the learning objectives and outcomes required, how goals will be segmented into modules or courses, and audience segmentation. The delivery component will ensure that an appropriate blend of delivery mechanisms is leveraged, such as simple e-learning, classroom-based training and performance support materials (eg quick reference cards and FAQs). To ensure the efficacy of the training delivered and ROI for the training initiative, a change manager may adopt an evaluation approach. Typical methods include the Kirkpatrick Evaluation Model and Kaufman's model (Downes, 2016). For example, Kirkpatrick's model provides a framework to evaluate training based on reaction, learning, performance and results.

- **Sponsor:** The sponsor is the person who is ultimately held accountable for the success of a project. A change manager can support the sponsor by identifying, mapping out and managing the sponsorship coalition. The change manager can prepare a sponsor roadmap for the sponsor, which outlines all of the sponsor's expected activities (eg events, communications, etc).

- **Resistance management:** A resistance management plan identifies how to manage the various resistance items that are encountered or likely to be encountered throughout the programme. Note that there can be an overlap between potential barriers identified and project risks.

- **Go-live assessment, readiness and support:** As a project heads towards go-live, a change manager will focus on assessing the readiness for change in the organisation using surveys, interviews and engagement, with a particular focus on the people side. This ensures that individuals and teams have the knowledge and ability to implement the change. On and around a go-live date, when people will typically get the 'wobbles', you might see change managers providing go-live support, eg by 'walking the floor'.

- **Sustaining and embedding:** In recent years, the change management profession has become increasingly aware that change managers need to be actively involved with the pre- and post-go-live business. This helps ensure that the change is sustained, ie it sticks. They will seek to understand what incentives are in place to sustain the change. Conversely, are there incentives or practices in place that might undermine the change or reduce the ROI (eg misaligned reward structures embedded in power bases)?

The following chapters will delve deeper into communications, learning, project management and how individuals in organisations respond to change.

5
Project Management

'A good plan today is better than a perfect plan tomorrow.'
— Proverb

According to the Project Management Institute (PMI), project management is 'the use of specific knowledge, skills, tools and techniques to deliver something of value to people. The development of software for an improved business process, the construction of a building, the relief effort after a natural disaster, the expansion of sales into a new geographic market—these are all examples of projects' (PMI, nd).

Project managers strive to add value, transparency and traceability to their projects. Good project managers avoid being seen as red tape or an extra burden. They apply an appropriate level of governance to each project depending on the scope, risk profile, budget, etc.

Expertise

Project managers tend to have expertise in dealing with plans, resources and data. They will typically adopt a structured approach to their work and are rewarded for delivering the project on time, on budget and within the agreed scope. We can contrast this with the competencies and approach adopted by change managers discussed in the previous chapter. Like change management, project management can be seen as a leadership and management competency, a body of knowledge and a profession.

It can be helpful to understand the distinction between projects and programmes. Projects tend to focus on outputs and typically last up to about a year. Programmes focus on capability building, tend to last longer than a year, and often consist of several projects.

Projects are commonplace in most organisations but how is project management relevant to a start-up? Understanding project management is critical to understanding what happens within organisations that use your product. It is possible that your product doesn't require a dedicated project to be implemented, but, in these circumstances, your product is likely part of a broader programme of work within your client's organisation. In addition, just like the change manager discussed in the previous chapter, a client's project manager is likely to be a key stakeholder. It can help to understand their perspective and terminology. For a start-up, you may also find you can apply project management approaches and principles to your product roadmap, internal operations or even the development of your core product.

History

At its core, project management is a simple concept. It's about the coordination and control of a group of people working towards a common goal. Let's start by looking back at the history of project management in the early twentieth century. Henry Gantt (1861–1919), a seminal figure in project management, is credited with the invention of what became known as Gantt charts. These charts, or scheduling diagrams, were significant as they recognised and displayed the importance of breaking projects down into smaller tasks and understanding the dependencies between tasks. Gantt charts played a significant role in completing the construction of the Hoover Dam in the US in the 1930s (Seymour & Hussein, 2014).

If you spend enough time with project managers, you are bound to hear someone mention the 'critical path'. In 1957, Morgan Walker of the DuPont Company and James Kelley of Remington Rand developed the critical path method (CPM). Using this technique, project managers can predict project duration by analysing which sequence of activities has the least scheduling flexibility. Then, when considering a delay for an activity, we first consider 'is it on the critical path?'. If it is, any delays to the activity will likely lead to delays in project completion. Conversely, activities not on the critical path have a greater degree of flexibility or slack. The development of this method is reputed to have saved DuPont over a million dollars in its first year (Haughey, 2010). And that was back in the 1950s when a million dollars meant quite a lot to a global corporation.

The next significant development in the modern history of project management was the work breakdown structure (WBS) established in the 1960s by the US Department of Defense and NASA, in connection with the US Navy's Polaris mobile submarine-launched ballistic missile project. A WBS is a hierarchical tree structure representing the deliverables, tasks and activities that need to be performed to successfully complete a project.

Modern approaches

In recent years, projects have tended to fall into one of two camps: waterfall or agile. Waterfall is the more traditional approach that emphasises a linear progression throughout a project and focuses on upfront planning and detailed documentation. The agile approach was developed in the 2000s by software developers who published the 'Manifesto for Agile Software Development' (Beck, 2001). Initially used exclusively in software development initiatives, it is now widely used on various types of projects. In the waterfall approach, features are fixed at the outset and there is a degree of flexibility with time and cost. Conversely, with agile, the time and cost tend to be set while there is flexibility regarding the final list of features to be delivered. Agile projects have a more iterative approach and greater emphasis on prioritising and re-prioritising features. If part of your launch strategy is to build a minimum viable product (MVP), you will probably use an agile approach.

Although agile is possibly the better-known approach nowadays, there are still some projects for which the waterfall approach will be the obvious and logical choice. If you are an engineer building a bridge, you won't need an MVP and you're more likely to adopt a waterfall project management approach.

We can best illustrate the day-to-day work of a project manager in the context of the three project constraints – scope (S), cost (C) and time (T) – or the 'project triangle' shown below.

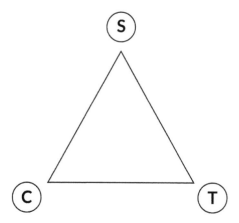

Figure 2 *Project constraints*

To achieve successful project outcomes, we need to be mindful of these three project constraints. They impact quality and all of the elements are interrelated, eg if you reduce cost (budget), you will impact the scope and quality. A project manager is constantly trying to find the right balance between the three project constraints while also delivering to the expected and agreed-on quality levels.

Projects are constantly faced with requests for new features (ie a change in scope) via a change request. Here the project manager's challenge is meeting the client's needs while ensuring all stakeholders are aware of the impact of budget and the schedule (ie cost or time).

Toolkit

To further understand project management, let's consider some of the essential tools and approaches used by project managers. These will help you understand and relate to project management folk in your customers' organisation or, indeed, you can use them when managing projects within your start-up.

- **Project brief:** The project brief is a core requirement and probably one of the first vital documents to be created when launching a project: 'It is used to provide a full and firm foundation for Initiating a Project' (OGC, 2009). It should contain details of project background, product description, objectives, desired outcomes, scope and exclusions, summary business case, and the intended approach. Having these documented and agreed to, and ideally formally signed off, can avoid frustration and confusion in later stages of the project when there will inevitably be misunderstandings and disagreements about the project's scope and intent. That does not imply that a project brief is cast in stone and can never be amended. This can be done, but it shouldn't be done lightly. It may be necessary if new senior stakeholders become involved with a project, key considerations change or important assumptions turn out to be wrong.

- **Project plan:** The plan 'provides a statement of how and when objectives are to be achieved, by showing the major products, activities and resources required for the scope of the plan' (OGC, 2009). It should contain prerequisites, external dependencies, planning assumptions, budgets, tolerances and a schedule.

- **Gantt chart:** As mentioned above, Gantt charts are some of the most valuable tools in the project manager's toolkit. They can help you visualise the tasks required to complete a project, their dependencies and the necessary resources. We have found them extremely useful for presenting a quick update to a client as you can highlight the status, critical path, key milestones and go-live date.

- **Managing risks and issues:** Successfully managing project risks and issues is critical to delivering a successful project. These risks and issues are often captured in a formal register, reviewed and regularly discussed throughout the project. PRINCE2 describes a risk as 'an uncertain event or set of events that, should it occur, will affect the achievement of objectives. It consists of a combination of the probability of a perceived threat or opportunity occurring, and the magnitude of its impact on objectives' (OGC, 2009).

  An issue is an item or event that has already occurred and needs to be addressed. This could be a risk that has turned into an issue. In less formal project management approaches, an issue could be anything that needs to be addressed by the project manager or project team. This could be a request to clarify the dates for training on a new system that could be entered into an issues register by the project team.

- **Budgets:** Budgets, or the cost project constraint, are central to a project manager's responsibilities. Many project managers will create and manage the budget for a project and will generally ensure there is a contingency for unknowns, eg a 10% buffer that may or may not be needed.

- **Status reports:** Project managers must regularly produce and present a project status report to key stakeholders, particularly project sponsors and steering committees. A good status report will include the project's current status, possibly using a traffic light approach, the key tasks and milestones for the current and upcoming period, an update on risks and issues and the current budget position.

- **Technology:** Although MS Project is still the go-to tool for most project managers, there is a proliferation of web-based project management applications and tools today (eg Asana, monday. com, Smartsheet and Wrike). AI will significantly impact project management in the coming years. In his book *Applying Artificial Intelligence to Project Management* (2019), Paul Boudreau explains how you can use machine learning to predict whether a particular project will be successful.

Behavioural science

Throughout this book, we emphasise the importance of understanding behavioural science insights as a start-up founder. Behavioural science can also help improve the project management process and is beginning to make inroads in this area. The Behavioural Insights Team (formerly an offshoot of the UK Cabinet Office, now independent of the UK government and owned by Nesta) has published a study conducted with the UK Department of Transport that investigated biases that impacted project management teams (Behavioral Insights Team, 2017). They found that three common cognitive biases affected decision-making and judgement within projects: optimism bias, sunk cost bias and groupthink.

We can see that project management should be a critical competency for any technologist. Specifically for start-ups, if this isn't a core competency for a founder, it certainly should be for one of the early hires.

6

How Disruptive Is Your Product?

'There is nothing more difficult to take in hand, more perilous to conduct, or more uncertain in its success than to take the lead in the introduction of a new order of things.'
— Niccolò Machiavelli, Italian diplomat, author and philosopher (Machiavelli, 1532)

In the early days of a tech B2B business, most founders concentrate on developing and fine-tuning their minimum viable product (MVP) and securing those initial customers that allow them to prove their value proposition and get a foothold in their market. While this is understandable, we feel there is a competitive advantage in considering a product's impact on users and organisations. Humans can deal with a finite amount of change before we become overwhelmed or burned out. Individuals overwhelmed by change shut out new ideas, including new products. Understanding the change load of your product at the earliest stage can significantly improve the chances of ongoing success for the product.

Many factors determine the success of any change initiative or technology project. At the individual level, these can include the type of individual and their experience with change, both at their current and previous employers. A team or organisation's track record of achieving change can be a significant factor at a broader level. While some of these factors are outside the control of any technology vendor, let alone a start-up, some factors can be influenced to greatly improve the chances of success for a tech B2B product's implementation in any organisation.

The Change Formula

What if you could use a formula to predict the likelihood of successfully implementing and adopting your product? We believe the Beckhard-Harris Change Formula provides a solid indicator of the change load introduced by your product. Originally described in the 1960s by management consultant David Gleicher, it was further developed by Richard Beckhard and Reuben T Harris in the 1980s (Beckhard & Harris, 1987). You will see different variations of the formula, but we prefer this version:

C = [ABD] > X

The Beckhard-Harris Change Formula

The Beckhard-Harris Change Formula states that for any change to be successful, factors A, B and D must outweigh the perceived cost of the change (X). Our three factors A, B and D are as follows:

A	Level of dissatisfaction with status quo
B	Desirability of proposed change or end state
D	Practicality of proposed change

When we consider the cost of change, we take into account the financial and emotional costs and the friction inherent in changing something that already exists. This also includes the contribution this change will make towards change saturation in the organisation.

While working on technology implementations, we've often found that although the users had no overt objection to the new system, they were very comfortable with their existing system and reluctant to move away from the legacy system to a new one. The user's level of dissatisfaction with the status quo (A) was low.

Low desirability (B) will occur when the features or benefits of new technology have not been clearly articulated or the 'what's in it for me?' (WIIFM) has not been made apparent to each stakeholder. Of course, there are also occasions when a product is simply impractical for an organisation either because the timing is not right or the product doesn't meet the client's requirements. This leads to low practicality of the proposed change (D).

The initial step in using the change formula to determine the likelihood of your product being successfully implemented and adopted in your client's organisation is to articulate all five elements of the formula. Can you do this for your product? You can conduct the exercise generically or ideally with a willing customer with whom you have a great relationship. The table below suggests questions under each heading to help articulate each item and get a gut feeling for whether the change formula predicts success for your product.

Questions to Ask

Beckhard-Harris Change Formula questions

	Change
	What is the driver for introducing this change?
C	Who are your stakeholders, and how does the change impact them?
	What are the success measures for the project?
	Level of dissatisfaction with status quo
A	Is there a legacy system or process that you are replacing?
	If so, how do users feel about the legacy system?

(continued)

Beckhard-Harris Change Formula questions (continued)

B	**Desirability of proposed change or end state** How well do the stakeholders understand the end state and how much do they want it? Can you articulate the WIIFM for each stakeholder?
D	**Practicality of proposed change** Is there a project plan in place? Has a sufficient budget been allocated to achieve successful implementation? Does the organisation have sufficient resources and commitment to implement the product successfully? (This could include the change management resources discussed at the start of this section.)
X	**Cost of change** Will implementation lead to change saturation for individuals using your technology? How much friction will this change cause users?

Once you have articulated and considered all the elements, you will have a good sense of how easy your product is to adopt and identified potential blockers. Inevitably, there will be instances where using the formula will indicate a low chance of success for your product, eg due to low dissatisfaction with the status quo. This might indicate that your project or product are just not suitable for the context, and it is always better to know this sooner rather than later.

We have developed a Change Formula Tool that enables you to quantify the strength of these elements and predict the likelihood of success in a relatively objective manner. Try the tool for free on our website (www.Humology.com/tools).

For tech founders in a competitive marketplace, you need to take advantage of all the useful tools you can to set yourself apart from the competition and grow your brand. The Change Formula is a great tool to have in your arsenal. Armed with these insights, you can adjust your product features, improve the way you implement your product and adapt how you communicate about your product.

7
Know Your Stakeholders

'You can please some of the people all of the time,
you can please all of the people some of the time,
but you can't please all of the people all of the time.'
— John Lydgate, fifteenth century monk and
poet (Gordon, 2018)

Managing stakeholders effectively is a crucial skill for anyone involved in business, especially for founders and entrepreneurs. You can apply this skill to tasks ranging from managing a project to launching a new product or service. Whether the stakeholder is a customer, supplier or someone you need to influence, managing stakeholders is a technical soft skill that will increase your chances of success in almost every endeavour.

The programme management methodology Managing Successful Programmes (MSP®) defines a stakeholder as 'any individual, group or organisation that can affect, be affected by or perceives itself to be affected by, a programme' (Office of Governance Commerce, 2007). We can replace programme here with project or any initiative (eg building a new product or service). We particularly like this definition as it reminds us that we need to focus not only on those who are genuinely impacted but also on those who perceive themselves to be impacted, whether rightly or wrongly (we hope we don't appear too judgemental here; everyone has a right to perceive that a change impacts them). The key message is to take a holistic view of all possible stakeholders. Remember, perception can be reality.

Essentially, we end up with three categories of stakeholder: those who are impacted by the initiative, those who can influence or affect the initiative, and finally, those who perceive that the initiative impacts them. We should also remember that stakeholders can be internal or external to the organisation where the change is occurring (eg unions or public authorities).

As a founder or entrepreneur, you may already have a clear understanding of your business's relevant stakeholders. This list typically includes customers and clients, partners, employees, vendors and suppliers, investors and bankers, advisors and influencers. This is a valuable and valid perspective; however, we apply a different lens in this chapter and look at stakeholders from another perspective. That is, who are the stakeholders that will make or break the success of your product or service? This should add to and reinforce the perspectives provided in previous chapters on how project management and change management work within your customers' organisations. Understanding the breadth of stakeholders in this way allows better communication with customers and a tailored approach to implementation and communications, resulting in the more successful implementation of your product or service.

Approach

As we'll explore in Chapter 24, modern consumers wish to engage with purpose-led organisations. After leading complex change management initiatives for over twenty years, we have devised a foolproof four-step approach to managing stakeholders no matter the project, culture or constituents. The four steps are:

1. **Identify:** The first step is identifying the stakeholders and conducting a change impact assessment. This assessment describes the significant changes in the initiative and how various stakeholders are impacted.

2. **Assess:** In the next step, we assess our stakeholders. We look to understand each stakeholder's interest or stake in the project, their influence, their support for the project and their key concerns and issues.

3. **Engage:** We determine the best way to communicate and engage with each stakeholder and then initiate these activities.

4. **Manage:** The final step is intended to encapsulate all of the above activities and the ongoing management of each stakeholder, ensuring that an appropriate person reaches out to a stakeholder to keep them aligned and committed to the initiative where relevant and needed.

Stakeholder matrix

One of the simplest yet most effective tools in stakeholder management is a stakeholder matrix. A typical version of this is an 'influence versus impact' matrix, where we plot the various stakeholders on a two-by-two matrix based on the level of influence they have over the initiative's success and how much they are impacted by the initiative, as illustrated in the following HR-related project example.

The value is not derived from putting the people precisely in the correct box but from thinking about and discussing who the stakeholders are and where we believe they sit to determine the right approach to engaging each stakeholder in the right way, with the right level of information, at the right times.

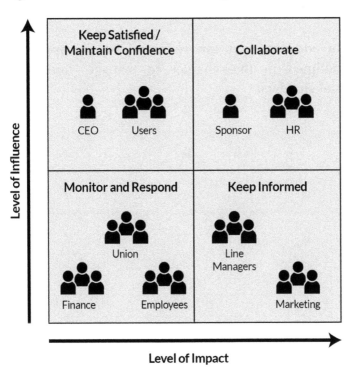

Figure 3 *Stakeholder matrix*

This brief insight into stakeholder management will allow you to understand the challenges your customers face as they navigate the various stakeholders within the organisation. Consider how you can assist your customers in navigating these challenges. Based on previous clients, can you help your customer with identifying stakeholders? Is there a way to adapt your implementation approach to ensure that all relevant stakeholders feel engaged with the process? Can you leverage stakeholder management to inform your sales and marketing strategy?

In addition, you can certainly use the approach outlined in this chapter to manage your own stakeholders.

8
Practice Makes Perfect

'Tomorrow's battle is won during today's practice.'
— Japanese Proverb

Consider the last time you underwent training in a corporate context. It is more likely to have been self-led e-learning or, if live, in a virtual classroom than formally in a face-to-face classroom environment. This trend was already evident before Covid-19 but has accelerated throughout the pandemic as we switched to conducting business in a virtual environment.

The recognition that training doesn't occur exclusively in a classroom setting prompted three researchers and authors (Morgan McCall, Michael M Lombardo and Robert A Eichinger) working with the

Center for Creative Leadership to create the 70:20:10 model for learning and development in the 1980s (Jennings, 2015). The three elements of the model are: 70% of learning is on the job, 20% of learning is social and 10% of learning is formal (otherwise known as 'on the job', 'near the job' and 'off the job'). The model's premise is that, in a modern workplace, training no longer takes place exclusively in a formal classroom situation; rather most training takes place informally on the job or socially within the organisation. They also argue that this is the most effective mix (ie on the job is much more impactful than off the job, particularly as it relates to the transfer of learning).

When a new technology is introduced to an organisation the learning and development (L&D) team will typically prepare an approach for training. The 70:20:10 model is a common approach but by no means the only one. While we're not advocating that your clients will need to divide up training on your product according to these exact proportions, the model does allow a good discussion about the best approach to help your clients learn how to use your product and ultimately adopt the technology. If you are only offering training courses on how to use your product, then no matter how good they are, you are only targeting 10% of the learning opportunity and your clients will probably be unimpressed.

70:20:10 learning model

Let's take a closer look at each of the model's components:

- **On the job (70%):** Includes learning from experience, problem-solving, incidental learning and practice. We might learn as we use a new system. An online help feature within the application or a quick reference guide could be included.

- **Social (20%):** Includes communities, networks, mentoring, coaching, sharing and collaboration. Imagine using a new expenses system for the first time. You ask a peer if they have already done something you don't know how to do in the new system. Taking a digital approach, there might be a discussion forum about the new system where users can post a question to colleagues.

- **Formal (10%):** Includes courses, classroom training, e-learning and virtual classrooms.

You might feel that today's technologies are expected to be completely intuitive and require no consideration of training. We urge technology providers not to be complacent when onboarding new users. As we'll explore in subsequent chapters, humans (technology users) are complex and full of surprises.

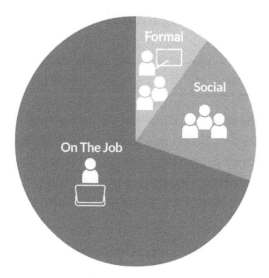

Figure 4 *70:20:10 training*

At the very least, user training and onboarding should be considered part of your product's core offering. Organisational learning and development teams may have a say on whether your product is chosen, regardless of the business function the product addresses – the effort required to adopt your product and the degree to which you support it may be a deciding factor.

Here are some questions to get you thinking about using this model for your product:

1. How will users or employees adapt to using your product/learn how to use your product?

2. Which of these approaches is relevant for you?

3. What will you do to make these approaches easier for your users and client organisations? (Product design and/or implementation approach.)

4. How will you evaluate the success of your training approach for each client and more generally?

Measurement

Now, let's take a look at two different methods you can use to measure your training approach's success and efficacy: the Kirkpatrick Evaluation Model and Prosci's ROI model.

Developed by Dr Donald Kirkpatrick in the 1950s, the Kirkpatrick Evaluation Model is probably the best-known model for analysing and evaluating the efficacy of training, particularly in the HR profession. As you progress through the four levels it can become increasingly difficult and time-consuming to gather appropriate information, even for seasoned HR professionals evaluating an internal training initiative. However, we believe it is a valuable model to consider how to measure and assess the efficacy of your approach to onboarding new users. Perhaps it is something you can use with a beta or select clients. The table below describes each of the four levels.

The Kirkpatrick Evaluation Model for training

Level	Description
Level 1	Reaction – this level measures the learner's reaction to the training. Typically, learners fill in attitude questionnaires or 'happy sheets' at the end of a course.
Level 2	Learning – this level assesses to what degree the learners acquired the intended knowledge, skills and behaviours from attending the learning event. Typically, a test or assessment can be performed at the end of the training or soon after training (eg online when the learners return to their desks).
Level 3	Performance – this level assesses to what extent learners are applying the newly acquired knowledge or skills on the job. In organisations, line managers will check this via observation.
Level 4	Results – this level assesses to what degree the agreed business outcomes were achieved because of the training. This can be considered the ROI to the organisation and is probably the hardest assessment to make. Outcomes can be affected by many factors (eg training efficacy, team culture and external factors). It can be hard to attribute a business outcome to a single factor.

Arguably, a more straightforward method to use is Prosci's ROI factors. Prosci, a global leader in change management solutions and certification, provides its three ROI factors to sell the benefits of a formal change management approach. Still, we feel that it can be easily applied to evaluating the efficacy of a training approach. The three factors are speed of adoption, proficiency and ultimate utilisation described in more detail below.

Prosci's model for measuring ROI of learning

Speed of adoption	How quickly can users get up to speed with the new technology?
	There is an inevitable productivity dip when adopting most new technologies, but we want that dip to be as shallow and short-lived as possible.
Proficiency	How proficient in the new technology are our users?
	Can they fully utilise the product as envisioned by the product founders?
	Are there a lot of support/help desk calls?
Ultimate utilisation	How many of the expected user population end up using the system?

So, what channels or mechanisms can you use to help your users get up to speed with your product? This is not a definitive list, but here are a few items to get you thinking:

- Infographics
- Recorded webinars
- Recorded screen captures

- Lunch and learn sessions for multiple clients, virtually or in person

We hope you can see from this discussion on training that it is something that a tech B2B start-up should address and indeed, in doing so, may gain a competitive advantage.

9

The SCARF Model

'The brain may devise/laws for the blood, but a hot temper leaps/o'er a cold decree'
— William Shakespeare, *Othello*
(Shakespeare, 1622)

Neuroscience experiments have shown us that the brain has a similar response to isolation or exclusion as it does to physical pain. The part of the brain associated with pain also lights up in an MRI machine when we feel isolated or excluded from a social situation.

The brain experiences the workplace as a social system. The modern workplace is a somewhat artificial construct, particularly when viewed in evolutionary terms. After all, our ancient ancestors didn't have an annual 360-degree performance review process to fret about. We can all relate to a change being 'sprung upon us', making us react defensively because we weren't consulted. We've also collectively been swept up in waves of change that make us feel good and part of something powerful (like global movements, the latest TikTok challenge or jumping on the latest app like Clubhouse). Why do we react negatively to some changes and positively to others?

David Rock developed the SCARF model in 2008 to help us understand how we behave in social situations, including the workplace (Rock, 2008). The SCARF elements represent the five key domains that influence our behaviour in these situations. SCARF is based on the idea that these domains trigger the same fundamental threat and reward response that we have always relied on for our physical survival. We move towards reward and away from threat. This is why we can have strong emotional responses in work situations and why it is not just a simple matter of switching those responses on or off. They are hardwired into our brains. The five elements are:

- **Status:** Our importance in relation to others.

- **Certainty:** Our ability to predict the future.

- **Autonomy:** Our perception of control over events.

- **Relatedness:** Our sense of belonging and safety with others.

- **Fairness:** Our perception of how fair exchanges between people are.

When an employee feels threatened, it reduces their ability to solve problems, think creatively and communicate effectively with others. We have all experienced stressful situations in the workplace when we could not think straight. Our reaction to stress is driven by cortisol – the stress hormone – kicking in.

Conversely, when we receive positive feedback or a leader provides a feeling of certainty in uncertain times, we sense this as a reward and move towards it. This leads to a happier and more productive workforce. Before we turn our attention to technology, let's get a better understanding of the model by looking at some everyday and work situations under the five SCARF headings. These are general considerations based on the average response, but all people are different and can behave in idiosyncratic ways.

Status

One of the reasons the performance review process can be challenging for many organisations is that it can provoke a threat response in employees and they may feel their status is threatened. Similarly, sometimes it is hard for us to receive advice or feedback as we feel that the other person is claiming superiority. This shouldn't be the case, but how often have we felt this way? Let's look at a threat example: the product replaces some of the tasks you do, eroding your sense of status. Conversely, the product will enable you to do your job more efficiently and eliminate errors, boosting your credibility with a reward.

Certainty

The human brain craves certainty. Without it, we automatically try to figure out what will happen next, stealing away neural energy from more productive activities. Providing a roadmap in uncertain times and breaking down complex projects are examples of how leaders in organisations can provide clarity.

Autonomy

Many of us will have experienced being micromanaged in the workplace. It is not a nice position to be in and can sap our enthusiasm. A perception of a lack of control or agency can lead to a threat response, elevating stress levels. Supplying employees with meaningful choices and the freedom to try out new ideas can stimulate the reward system in the brain.

Relatedness

As humans, we are social animals and like building relationships and forming groups. A lack of relatedness can lead to feelings of isolation and loneliness, which reduce creativity and collaboration. To help develop a feeling of relatedness, leaders should encourage collaboration, open communication and team-building activities.

Fairness

A perception of unfairness can generate adverse reactions. Studies have shown that people are more satisfied with a fair exchange that offers minimal reward than an unfair exchange that offers a large reward. Leaders can reduce the likelihood of unfairness by making sure that rules, norms and expectations for teams are set and clear.

The SCARF model helps understand how potential users or buyers perceive technology. With a threat response, users will move away from your product, leading to low utilisation and sales of your product. With a reward response, users will move towards a product leading to increased utilisation and better product adoption, less friction and ultimately increased sales and enhanced brand reputation.

Let's look at the five elements of SCARF again, this time through the lens of B2B tech products.

SCARF model

Status	Consider how your product's implementation will impact the status of stakeholders in your client's organisation. Managers might perceive that their status is particularly affected by new technology. Consider the example of implementing an AI or robotic process automation (RPA) system. Managers may perceive that this will reduce the amount of control over their teams and their status within the organisation. If this occurs, it might be because you, or your client, haven't articulated the benefits of your product (ie the WIIFM), which hopefully will outweigh any perception of loss of status.
Certainty	Avoid generating uncertainty for your users wherever you can. Tell them what's just happened, what's happening now and what's happening next. If users can see where a transaction is in the workflow, they feel more in control. For example, an expense system and the approval workflow contained in it.
Autonomy	Encourage your users' sense of freedom and autonomy by allowing them to experiment safely with your product (eg in a sandpit environment). Can you backtrack out of a transaction easily and intuitively in the live environment? Does it make the user feel empowered to try again or would they feel punished?

(continued)

SCARF model (continued)

Relatedness	Is your product increasing or decreasing an employee's sense of relatedness and belonging? Can you improve this by making it easier for users to communicate with other users, either within or outside the organisation? This might be via a communication channel like Slack, a Facebook group or as part of a product user group, where they can exchange ideas with users from other organisations.
Fairness	From a B2B tech product perspective, avoiding the perception of unfairness probably boils down to how you communicate about your product and how your product is implemented in a client's organisation.
	Admittedly, some of this will be out of your control, but you can encourage and support your client with open and transparent communication. Can you nudge your client to include fair representation from across the enterprise when planning the implementation of your product?
	Technologists have the opportunity to minimise threats and maximise rewards for their most important stakeholders by adjusting product features, how the product is implemented and key product messages.

PART THREE

Designing With Humans In Mind

10

The Gatekeepers
To The Brain

'Civilization advances by extending the number of
important operations which we can perform without
thinking of them.'
— Alfred North Whitehead, English
mathematician (Whitehead, 1911)

Rapid growth in technologies has changed the way
we learn, work and connect with each other. Technology is now intimately and inextricably entwined
in our everyday lives, reshaping how we experience
the world around us. At its best, it has stretched our
imaginations and capabilities beyond our expectations. At its worst, it has reflected our most shameful
behaviours and shone a spotlight on our inner biases –
revealing our darkest thoughts, intentions and fears.
As we sprint to keep up, we're finding ourselves in
an evolutionary arms race between humanity and

technology. Unfortunately, there are no winners in an arms race, only collateral damage.

Over the past decade, we have witnessed the quiet repositioning of Big Tech from its traditional position as humanity's servant to its present, and more ominous, role of master and commander. Without deliberate action, the evolutionary gap between technology and humanity will continue to expand, leaving the majority behind. Humans differ from machines in the most fundamental ways – we're intuitive, our limited processors are not easily upgraded, and we are hardwired to choose the path of least effort. In short, we favour easy over effort, comfort over change and now over later.

Keeping pace in a noisy accelerated world is like trying to listen to a whisper in a loud group of people – it demands the concentrated effort of both parties. We believe a fundamental understanding of human information processing can help us build tools that do not require humans to radically adopt new behaviours or adapt to the changing world around them. Armed with this knowledge, we can build better products and services that are designed with humans in mind.

Attention and working memory: The brain's gatekeepers

A human brain processes billions of data points every second, making lightning-fast decisions about what is important and filtering out unnecessary noise. This sophisticated filtering system prevents us from being overwhelmed by the sheer volume of shiny new objects vying for our limited attention and enables us to focus on a limited number of inputs. Even then, once we've determined what we need to pay attention to, our brains are further constrained by the limitations of our working memory.

When we listen to a set of directions or hold a person's name in mind as they introduce themselves, we rely on our working memory to retain and recall chunks of information while we gather and make sense of the entire message being delivered to us. In this way, working memory acts like a gatekeeper to the brain, protecting us from overwhelm. For technologists, working memory holds the keys to the kingdom, and it is *very* selective about what gets past the door.

In his much-cited paper 'The magical number seven, plus or minus two: Some limits on our capacity for processing information', cognitive psychologist George Miller estimated that we can hold between five and nine individual items in our working memory at any one time (Miller, 1956). This concept is known as Miller's Law. More recently, Nelson Cowan found that four units plus or minus one might be more realistic (Cowan, 2001). Much of this research explains why phone numbers are often seven digits and more recently PIN codes are only four digits.

We also clear our 'mental cache' regularly as a decluttering exercise. New information is held in working memory for only a few seconds, with almost all information lost after about twenty seconds. It's hard to believe that humans continue to achieve so much with such a tight bottleneck at the entrance to the brain's enormous capacity. These constraints are central to our cognitive architecture, affecting each of us as we go about our daily lives.

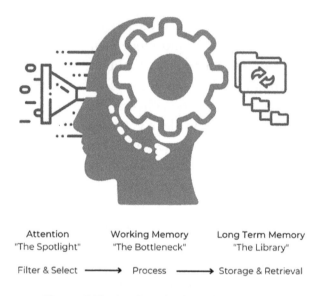

| Attention | Working Memory | Long Term Memory |
| "The Spotlight" | "The Bottleneck" | "The Library" |

Filter & Select ⟶ Process ⟶ Storage & Retrieval

Figure 5 *The bottleneck of working memory*

Let's try a short experiment. Take a look at the letters below briefly, then write down (or recite) as many of them as you can in ten seconds:

ETHYSLIBGEH

Perhaps you fit squarely into Miller's Law or perhaps you didn't process more than three. The capacity you have for this task depends heavily on what else is going on in your head at the time. Whatever the outcome, the key message is that limited information passes through the bottleneck of working memory.

Let's try another task. Take a good look at the selection of words below, then write down (or recite) as many as you can remember:

TAT SAT MIT MOT HAT CAT TIP BAT PIP PAT

How many words could you recall in this task?

Congratulations – by grouping bits of data together, you just recalled three times the number of data inputs. This system of grouping, or 'chunking', is an effective way to optimise knowledge transfer and retention. Chunking involves grouping bits of data into blocks of information that are optimised for cognitive processing. Organising information in this way helps us make sense of the data before us and aids the easy and quick retrieval of information. For example, a chunked phone number +1-345-678-9012 is significantly easier to recall than an un-chunked phone number +13456789012.

Similarly, the words CAT, SAT and HAT are easier to remember due to our familiarity with them. Our brains have reference data for the word CAT that includes words like animal, feline, black, green eyes, four legs, etc. This dataset is called a schema. Familiar data is processed and stored faster because we can associate it with an existing schema, whereas new data, or a novel idea, requires more processing capacity to commit it to long-term memory.

The amount of information the working memory can hold at any one time is called the *cognitive load*. When the load is light, information passes through working memory with ease and gets stored in our long-term memory. When the load is dense, the process feels effortful. Just as running too many apps at once will slow your phone down, our brain begins to shut out new information as we approach our maximum cognitive load.

The challenge with humans is that while we can quickly and cheaply upgrade technology, humans do not (yet) come with expandable RAM. Even the most powerful minds have limited capacity to digest new information and a heavy cognitive load or a wave of complex demands can push our cognitive architecture beyond its limit. If we think of our brain like a sponge, cognitive load is the amount of water the sponge can retain before it becomes overwhelmed and begins to leak.

Designing for cognitive load

Faced with a wide selection of easy-to-use and free alternatives, frustrated users will follow the path of least effort, making cognitive load a key influencer in how users choose and adopt new technologies and apps. While we can't eliminate cognitive load completely (after all, users seek out products to solve a pain point), our aim is to minimise load and maximise knowledge transfer. In studying how humans process information, Australian educational psychologist John Sweller developed Cognitive Load Theory (CLT) as a framework for designing optimal learning experiences (Sweller, 2011). CLT addresses cognitive load in three distinct categories:

1. **Intrinsic load:** This refers to the intrinsic complexity of the task being undertaken. Think of it as the effort involved in learning a foreign language, as compared to joining a new Slack community. According to Sweller, 'intrinsic cognitive load can only be altered by changing the nature of what is learned or by the act of learning itself'. Hence understanding a user's prior knowledge, capacity for learning and aptitude can influence design.

2. **Extraneous load:** This is the load generated by the way the material is presented to a user and is independent of the task itself. Language, visual clutter, method of delivery, coherence, feedback, uncertainty and task progression fall within this category. UX designers are laser-focused on reducing this form of cognitive load.

3. **Germane load:** This refers to the mental energy needed to process information and depends on how that information is structured. The role of an instructional designer is to maximise knowledge

transfer to a learner with minimum cognitive effort using techniques such as chunking and rightsizing challenges.

As a rule of thumb, we should *manage* intrinsic load, *minimise* extraneous load and *maximise* germane load. Understanding your user, their current beliefs, existing knowledge, influencers and social norms is therefore central to designing a product that feels familiar and easy to use. Strategies to reduce cognitive load include:

- Optimise for knowledge transfer:

    - Employ chunking techniques

    - Group related objects together

    - Leverage the user's existing schema

    - Explore mental hooks that help the brain pay attention and help organise the information into logical schemas

    - Use TL;DR versions where appropriate[11]

- Less is more:

    - Eliminate non-essential details and distractions

    - Establish the path of least effort and follow it

    - Use defaults to reduce choice anxiety

---

11 TL;DR is a common internet acronym for 'Too Long; Didn't Read'. It refers to a summarised version of longer-form content aimed at our attention-poor society.

- Sense-making:

  - Avoid visual inconsistencies. Nest common items together (such as social media icons, formatting buttons)

  - Avoid clutter; eliminate repetition and redundancy, irrelevant or complex language and visual chaos

  - Use recognisable visual cues like icons and bullet points

  - Make clickable objects obvious – buttons, hyperlinks, play buttons, edit icons

- Establish flow:

  - User flow should be intuitive, consistent and progressive

  - Break complex tasks into smaller steps or hierarchies with logical sequences

  - Avoid task interruption

Interaction cost

When we interact with a new piece of technology for the first time, we quickly weigh up the effort required to derive value from a product. While this measure of interaction cost may seem crude and overly simplistic, it can significantly influence perceived usability, and hence a product's success. If a user finds a piece of technology intuitive and easy to navigate, they're likely to use the product again and again. High interaction costs, however, trigger anxiety and feelings of stress which are known to reduce our working memory capacity even further. Using cognitive load as a proxy for mental effort, and usability as a proxy for interaction cost, we can begin to paint a picture of how a user makes a crude assessment of usability. Why is this important? Because first impressions last.

Usability = derived value – cognitive load

Great products focus on maximising value delivered *and* minimising cognitive load. When both elements are optimised, users will engage with the product again and again.

Maximum usability = high user engagement

11
Consciously Unconscious

'Our life is frittered away by detail...Simplicity, simplicity, simplicity!'
— Henry David Thoreau, American naturalist and essayist (Thoreau, 1854)

First impressions really do matter. Every day we make thousands of split-second judgements. You might assume that our brains contain sophisticated machinery to carefully assess the inputs available to us, come up with a range of potential outcomes and make informed decisions. The reality is that most decisions or choices we make in life are based on heuristics – rules of thumb that were developed to preserve energy rather than enable effective decision-making.

It may come as a shock that 95% of our thoughts, emotions and learning occur without our conscious awareness (Zaltman, 2003). If we had to concentrate on every little thing we do in our lives, from tying our shoes to driving to work, we'd quickly exhaust our limited mental resources. Instead, as we progress through our lives, we use rules of thumb to approximate good enough outcomes. In this mode of thinking, most of our actions and thoughts happen without effort, intent or even awareness. Satisficing enables us to live by the motto 'progress over perfection'.

We are creatures of habit, preferring consistency over chaos. When our environment feels consistent, the association engine in our brain is in full flight, making fast connections and drawing lightning-quick conclusions that make us feel good about ourselves and the world around us. The more often we engage in a particular process the more our behaviour becomes habitual. Our most habitual processes are unintentional, efficient, autonomous and unconscious. However, they are also prone to error and loaded with inherent bias. Thankfully, just like the autopilot in an autonomous vehicle, we can hand over the controls when we come across terrain that is unfamiliar, unpredictable or requires skill to navigate.

Dual drivers

In his seminal book *Thinking, Fast and Slow,* Daniel Kahneman popularised the concept of dual drivers steering our daily thoughts and decisions (Kahneman, 2012). Kahneman divides the brain into two agents, System 1 and System 2, which respectively produce fast and slow thinking. System 1 operates automatically and quickly, with little or no effort and no sense of voluntary control. In contrast, System 2 rests on standby until called for. When operating effectively, System 2 will quickly grab hold of the controls and prevent System 1 from blurting out a cutting retort to your nemesis or replying to that email from an army veteran stranded abroad who urgently needs your bank details to wire funds to his starving family.

Familiarity breeds trust

A symbiotic relationship between System 1 and System 2 is critical – autopilot needs to know when to call for assistance and our conscious thinking mind needs to know when to take over the controls. In the human context, this decision tree is primarily based on previous experiences and what we believe to be true about the world we've experienced to date. System 1 cycles through a checklist to determine if System 2 is needed:

- Does the information presented MAKE SENSE to me?

- Is it CONSISTENT with what I know and understand about my world?

- Does it feel FAMILIAR? Can I TRUST it?

If the answer is YES to all of the above, System 2 endorses System 1 to continue and goes back into energy-saving 'sleep' mode. In this mode, we are at *cognitive ease*.

If the answer is NO to any of the above, an alert is passed to System 2 to step in. When System 2 is called on, intuition turns to scepticism, the unconscious becomes conscious and we experience *cognitive strain* (often described in the tech design world as friction).

For ease of recall, we'll use the following 'formulae':

C3 = Cognitive Ease

COHERENT + CONSISTENT + COMFORTABLE = COGNITIVE EASE

I3 = Cognitive Strain

INCOHERENT + INCONSISTENT + IRRITATED = COGNITIVE STRAIN

Figure 6 *Cognitive ease versus cognitive strain*

When we're at cognitive ease, we are unavoidably gullible and impressionable. In this state, we're pretty naive and willing to accept the information in front of us. We're likely to be in a good mood, believe information to be true and trust our instincts.

When System 2 is engaged, we are more likely to be vigilant and suspicious, invest more effort in what we're doing and make fewer errors. However, we're also less intuitive and creative than usual. This state of heightened awareness burns mental energy, physically exhausts us and leads to cognitive strain. In this state, we often hear people say 'my brain hurts' and 'this project is giving me a headache' – this is how cognitive friction feels. It creates tension within our attention.

Numerous psychological studies (several of which are described in great detail in *Thinking, Fast and Slow*) have identified various stimuli that cause us to switch from cognitive ease to cognitive strain. For example, reading complicated instructions, listening to simultaneous conversations, viewing text in too-small font or with poor contrast, and even being in a bad mood all generate cognitive strain.

When something becomes hard to think about, we transfer the discomfort of the thought to the object of our thinking. This matters because when friction is experienced, humans will blame the product, not their own cognitive capacities. We all know that, when confronted with effort, we find ways to avoid it or take a shortcut. Therefore, the direct result of eroding the user's self-confidence is less engagement with your product or service. A confused mind can't decide and a confused user won't engage.

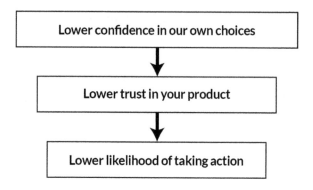

Figure 7 *The link between user confidence and taking action*

Like it or not, we are biologically hardwired to follow the path of least effort. We will, whenever possible, choose ease over effort and comfort over discomfort. Our brain's autopilot system is a beautiful energy-efficient engine that allows us to carry out a set of sequential tasks without expending much effort, saving our energy for more complex decisions ahead. Does that mean we are lazy or sloth-like? We don't believe so – we like to use the term 'cognitively efficient'.

Our brains' inclinations towards shortcuts and biases are both essential and wildly detrimental, depending on circumstance and application. If we're unscrupulous or careless in applying this knowledge, we can actively harm and alienate vulnerable people. Our responsibility as technologists lies first and foremost in the facilitation, protection and agency of our users. This is increasingly important as tech infiltrates more and more aspects of human life.

The role of habit

Habits reduce cognitive load and free up mental capacity for more complex thinking. Habits are simply behaviours that we repeat frequently over time. Therefore, how we behave is an indication of the type of person we believe ourselves to be. Once we adopt an identity, we can find it very hard to change our sense of self. Behaviours that are inconsistent with our identity are unlikely to stick around long enough to become habitual. We might dream of being the next Elon Musk or Jeff Bezos, but if we see ourselves as bad with money or lacking follow-through, we are unlikely to reach the lofty heights we aspire to.

Habits are formed from repeated experience. If something works out well, we're likely to do it again. The positive outcome acts as a reward, encouraging us to use the same formula when we encounter a similar situation in the future. In *Atomic Habits* (2018), James Clear breaks down the process of habit formation into four distinct steps:

1. **Cue:** The cue triggers your brain to initiate behaviour – a cue is alerted when we sense a reward is close.

2. **Cravings:** At this point, we are craving the reward or the outcome, not the process itself. We don't crave that glass of wine because we're thirsty; typically we're seeking the sense of relaxation or indulgence that it delivers.

3. **Response:** If the craving is strong enough, we move into the response mode. Whether we take action or not depends on how motivated we are and how much friction is associated with the behaviour. We'll discuss this process in more detail in Chapter 18.

4. **Reward:** If we are motivated enough to follow through, we savour the reward, completing the habit cycle.

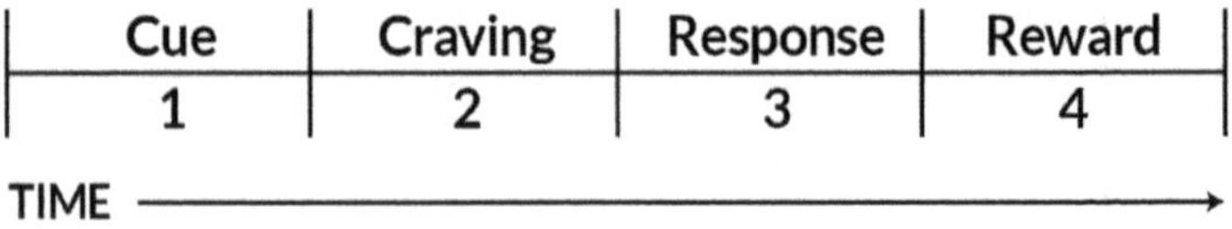

Cue	Craving	Response	Reward
1	2	3	4

TIME ────────────────────────────────→

Figure 8 *The science of how habits work*[12]

The relevance of habits and behaviours to technologists will become clear over the next few chapters. Too often, technology design requires users to behave in ways that are inconsistent with their existing habits and self-image. Where gaps exist between the user's current behaviours and the behaviours required to derive value from a piece of technology, we can decide to change the product or change the user behaviour. However, be warned: engaging in technology-led behaviour change requires a commitment of time and resources. We'll circle back to this aspect in Chapter 26.

Humans are a wonderful blend of evolutionary instincts, predispositions and cognitive biases that govern our thoughts and behaviours. While these traits can be positive and advantageous for our species – like our tendency to adopt social norms or our instinctual attention to fear and danger – they are also vulnerabilities we must explore, as they are easily hijacked in a world of increasing technological power.

12
Goldilocks And The Four-Letter Word

'The pleasure of change is opposed by that of habit; and if we love best that to which we are accustomed, we like best that which is new.'
— Letitia Elizabeth Landon, English poet and novelist (Landon, 1831)

In a world fuelled by the most incredible technological advances that we've seen over generations, it's increasingly hard to stand out. Many wonderful artists remain undiscovered, thousands of books go unread and lots of promising start-ups fail. While emerging technologies open up a world of discovery and opportunity for entrepreneurs, the pace of development has created a noisy marketplace for consumers. Faced with overwhelming choice, consumers are seeking an instant connection and a short time-to-value. Just as investors make high-stakes bets on where to invest their money, consumers gamble on where to invest their limited mental budget.

This is the modern entrepreneur's dilemma – the battle between the 'shiny object syndrome' inherent in entrepreneurs and creative types and the 'memory foam syndrome' of almost everyone else. While these syndromes are not medical terms, they are common enough conditions to offer valuable insights for technologists. *Shiny object syndrome* represents our tendency to be distracted by every new trend. In contrast, *memory foam syndrome* refers to our tendency to favour what we know over uncertainty – we are, quite simply, creatures of habit.

The Goldilocks principle

The tension between two opposing forces – neophilia (a love of new things) and neophobia (a fear of new things) – is at the heart of all innovation. Neophiliacs have a passion for novelty and exploration, while even the slightest disruption can trigger fear and resistance in neophobiacs. Realistically, everyone sits somewhere along the spectrum of neophilia to neophobia; each having a slight preference for newness or nostalgia. As a technologist, knowing where stakeholders are situated on this spectrum is critical to the success of your product.

Suppose your product is a disruptive innovation (that is, it requires your user to change their behaviours or habits) and your user profile edges towards neophobia. Your product strategy should aim to deliver the future in easily digestible chunks. If your product is disruptive and your user profile is more neophiliac, rock out the latest buzzwords and features and make sure you keep it surprising and exciting. After all, your users won't stick around if the buzz wears off. Understanding our relative preference for newness should continually inform the product roadmap and prioritisation of feature design.

Just like the classic fairy tale in which Goldilocks enters the house of the Three Bears, each time she samples their porridge, chairs and beds, she chooses the one that's 'just right'. Applying the Goldilocks principle to product development means finding that sweet spot that feels 'just right' for users depending on their preference for novelty or familiarity. It should not be so simple that it's boring or so unfamiliar that it's too alien or complex.

Figure 9 *Goldilocks spectrum*

The four-letter word

We would argue that one man understood the delicate dance between familiarity and novelty better than any other. Known as the father of industrial design, Raymond Loewy's designs are etched into twentieth-century American culture. From the Lucky Strike cigarette package to the Exxon logo to the blue nose of Air Force One, Loewy and his firm's designs often defined the times. Loewy became a cultural trendsetter for mid-century America, designing International Harvester tractors, Frigidaire ovens and Singer vacuum cleaners.

Loewy held a central belief that consumers gravitate towards products that are bold, yet instantly comprehensible. He called his grand theory the 'Most Advanced Yet Acceptable' or 'MAYA' Principle. This simple four-letter word beautifully captures the subtle tension between novelty and familiarity. As humans, we are hardwired to evolve – we only need to look back at what we've achieved in a single generation to witness how hard we strive for progress. Yet, we also fear change – another great paradox of humanity. The promise of progress fuels our motivation while our preference for familiarity acts as a brake to curb our enthusiasm. Just like Goldilocks, we gravitate to the middle – not too advanced, not too predictable, just the right degree of discovery.

Ultimately, we prefer innovative things to be derivatives (or incremental innovations) of things we are already familiar with. This partiality we have for familiarity is called the *mere exposure effect* – simply being exposed to a concept, the look or feel of a product, or a message, makes it more acceptable to us. Popular culture has long exploited the advantage of the familiar surprise – from timeworn archetypes in box office smashes like *Star Wars* and the Marvel hero movies, to remastered music albums and boyband comeback tours. Well-established characters with updated dialogue act out standard hero–villain storylines designed to entertain more than to educate. The twists and turns along the journey are always careful not to drift too far from the familiar.

The same concept can easily be applied to fashion, storylines, concepts and music. When Adele released her hotly anticipated single 'Easy on Me' in 2021, she was careful to ensure a consistent tone to bridge from her last album six years earlier. Accompanying her latest melodramatic power ballad is a black and white video showing the singer packing up the same house that she appeared to move into in her 2015 smash 'Hello'.

We delight in the thrill of a familiar story with a fresh twist. It denotes a sense of comfort and lets us know that the world around us is safe and makes sense. Connecting new attributes to old schemas also delights our associative autopilot mode of thinking. In this zone, we easily conflate the pleasure of the thought with the quality of the idea. Suddenly, something that feels right seems like the perfect choice to us. The start-up world is no stranger to this concept – Airbnb was once called 'eBay for homes', Uber and Lyft were considered 'the Airbnb of cars', and a generation of start-ups have pitched themselves as 'the Uber of...' (Thompson, 2017).

Many disruptive innovations pave the way for better versions to emerge once the concept has achieved market acceptance. In the search engine war, Yahoo created familiarity, but it was Google who led on usability and engagement. Friendster created the idea of connecting online with friends, but Facebook made it more accessible and scalable. Apple was not the first to release a tablet, portable MP3 player or even the touchscreen smartphone, but it excelled at human-centric design.[13]

There's also nothing new about taking photos; we've done it for centuries. However, the introduction of the first commercial camera phone in 1999 propelled our love of photography from 80 billion photos a *year* in 1999 to 80 billion a *month* by 2019. The availability of digital photographs spurred Mark Zuckerberg to iterate on his first product offering 'FaceMash' in 2003. Later, Facebook encouraged us to share our photos and have them validated by people who matter to us. Instagram enabled us to beautify those photographs with filters and assign them searchable tags. New business models sprouted and influencer marketing erupted – creating the perfect storm for TikTok's rise to the top. Each iteration is associated with a cultural micro-shift and represents an evolution from something familiar.

So, how do we make a product appear both novel and familiar at the same time? Too much novelty risks mainstream rejection, while introducing something very familiar won't engage users enough to switch from the status quo. Striking the right balance is even more challenging when introducing genuinely disruptive products to a mainstream audience.

---

13 Microsoft released its Tablet PC in 2001, almost a decade before Apple's iPad; in 1998, South Korea's SaeHan Information Systems created the first portable digital audio player, MPMan; and IBM invented the first touchscreen smartphone in 1994.

Overcoming this hurdle is what Geoffrey Moore referred to as 'crossing the chasm' in the title of his 1991 book (Moore, 1991). The 'chasm' represents the gap between two groups: those who have adopted new technologies (early adopters) and those who have yet to do so (the majority). The early majority are pragmatic and practical – they need an idea to be tried and tested before it piques their interest.

Overnight successes like Instagram and TikTok may appear disruptive, but each one represents a well-timed exploitation of the MAYA principle. Equally, Netflix's success was fuelled by the widespread adoption of streaming services and it capitalised on its data-gathering strategy by showing consumers recommendations based on what they and others had watched before – offering every consumer a personalised yet familiar surprise.

> **RULE 1: Inject novelty into something familiar, or inject familiarity into something novel.**
>
> **RULE 2: Deliver the future gradually. If it's disruptive, chunk it up into digestible nuggets of optimal newness.**

13
Psychological Approaches To Change

'The reasonable man adapts himself to the world:
the unreasonable one persists in trying to adapt the
world to himself. Therefore, all progress depends on
the unreasonable man.'
   — George Bernard Shaw, Irish playwright and
      polemicist, *Man and Superman* (Shaw, 1903)

In this chapter, we turn our attention to psychology and, in particular, we look at four of the most common psychological approaches to change in the workplace: behavioural, cognitive, psychodynamic and humanistic. These four critical approaches to guiding people through change are outlined in Cameron and Green's book *Making Sense of Change Management* (Cameron & Green, 2015). They also underpin many of the key concepts explained throughout this book.

The field of psychology has contributed significantly to the advancement of the change management discipline and it is a pivotal contributor to behavioural design.

Behavioural approach

The behavioural approach to change focuses on how one individual can change another individual's behaviour using reward and punishment to achieve intended results. Proponents of this approach feel that 'all behaviours are acquired through conditioning' and 'only observable behaviour should be considered' (Cherry, 2021).

In the 1890s, Russian physiologist Ivan Pavlov conducted experiments in which dogs were conditioned to associate the ticking of a metronome with the arrival of food. Before long, Pavlov was able to elicit the desired response from the dog (ie salivation) by introducing the ticking metronome stimulus without the presence of food (McLeon, 2021). This observation is now referred to as classical conditioning.

The behaviourist view of the world eventually led to difficulties getting people to exhibit the 'right' behaviours. In 1960, in his book *The Human Side of Enterprise* in which he set out to explain employee motivation in the workplace, Douglas McGregor put forward his Theory X and Theory Y (McGregor, 1960). Theory

X assumes that you need to keep tight control over employees as they are generally not motivated to work, seeing it as merely a means to an end such as earning money and paying bills. Conversely, Theory Y assumes that people view work as a normal and healthy part of life and, given the right surroundings, are more than happy to be creative and hardworking and help an organisation achieve its goals. Theory Y also assumes that individuals desire rewards that satisfy their self-esteem and self-actualisation needs.

Cognitive approach

While behaviourists focused on observable behaviours, cognitive psychologists sought to understand the human capacity for learning and problem-solving. The cognitive approach focuses on how the internal mind works to influence behaviour (Atomi, 2019) and proposes that 'our emotions and our problems are a result of the way we think' (Cameron & Green, 2015).

Three assumptions drive all theories in this approach: limited capacity, control mechanism and two-way flow. Proponents of the cognitive approach believe that our brains can only process a certain amount of information at any given moment. They also believe that a superior part of the brain can control other parts of the brain and that the brain has input and output flows. In much the same way as a computer operates, the brain takes input from the external environment, processes it and produces an output (ie a behaviour). Strategies used in the cognitive approach include affirmations, positive listings, reframing and visualisations (Cameron & Green, 2015).

Psychodynamic approach

The psychodynamic approach is based on the belief that we experience a series of psychological states when we are faced with changes in our external world (Cameron & Green, 2015). Sigmund Freud was a leading figure in this field. His psychodynamic theory proposed that most mental activity takes place outside of our conscious awareness and that our unconscious motivation influences our thoughts, feelings, and personality. He believed that the unconscious parts of our mind – the identity, the ego and the superego – are always in conflict with each other, which determines who we are (Course Hero, 2019).

Freud also introduced us to the eponymous Freudian slip, when someone accidentally says something that reveals their unconscious feeling. If you have ever called a friend or partner by the wrong name or called your teacher 'Mum', you will be familiar with these slips.

Swiss psychiatrist Kübler-Ross realised that, given the necessary conditions, terminally ill patients would typically go through five stages as they came to terms with their prognosis: denial, anger, bargaining, depression and finally acceptance. The model is discussed in Chapter 4. Some business and change management practitioners and consultants still use the model too literally. If you implement a new accounts payable system and users are experiencing anger and depression, you have more significant problems than a new IT system.

Virginia Satir developed her process of change model based on her work with individuals and families experiencing significant changes (Satir et al, 1991). Her model starts with the status quo and then a change occurs, or a 'foreign element' is introduced. An example in the workplace might be where new ways of working are brought in. This results in a period of chaos that persists until a 'transforming idea' is introduced, either from deep within an individual or by a third party (eg a counsellor or, in the case of a workplace change, a leader or change manager). This transforming idea might be an individual realising that these new ways of working are helping the team work more effectively and producing better results. We begin to accept the idea and a new status quo is born.

Humanistic approach

The humanistic approach to psychology emerged in the 1950s and 1960s in the US. The US Association for Humanistic Psychology describes this approach as 'concerned with topics having little place in existing theories and systems: eg love, creativity, self, growth... self-actualization, higher values, being, becoming, responsibility, meaning... transcendental experience, peak experience, courage and related concepts' (Cameron & Green, 2015).

Proponents of this theory believe that individuals have free will and can achieve self-actualisation. Contrasted with Freud's psychodynamic theory, which was deterministic (ie our unconscious desires determine our behaviour), the humanistic approach focuses on the conscious and assumes people are essentially good and self-motivated to improve.

The first key theorist of this approach was Abraham Maslow. In the 1940s, he created his hierarchy of needs shown below, which depicts how humans need to meet several more basic needs before reaching the highest state of self-actualisation (Maslow, 1943).

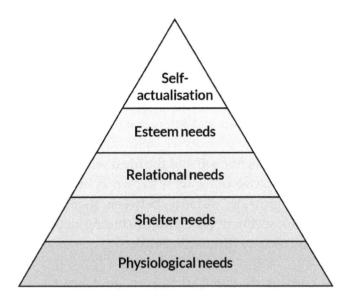

Figure 10 *Maslow's hierarchy of needs*

Few people reach the highest level of the hierarchy of needs – in fact, Maslow posited that only 1% could do so. Individuals who reach this state are incredibly self-aware and tend to focus their energy on a particular problem that becomes their life's work (Khan Academy, nd). We can think of several well-known historical figures who have reached this level, including Martin Luther King, Jr, Mother Teresa and Albert Einstein. Interestingly, Einstein was one of the eighteen people Maslow studied to develop his theory.

The second critical theorist in this area was Carl Rogers, who believed that the road to self-actualisation is a constant process that must take place in a growth-promoting environment (Khan Academy, nd). He also believed we are born with a whole true self, but as we grow up and interact with others and our environment over time, we split into two different parts: the authentic self and the ideal self. The separation of these two elements is known as incongruence and the growing distance between them is what causes us so many problems, including depression, fear and anxiety (Bruntsch, 2018).

We particularly like Carl Rogers' guidance for consultants and change agents about how to facilitate the growth and development of employees in an organisation. He advised that for the change agent to be effective, they need to be genuine and congruent, and have unconditional, positive regard with empathic understanding.

This chapter has looked at behavioural, cognitive, psychodynamic and humanistic approaches to bringing about change in individuals. We are sure you will appreciate how these important concepts contributed to the development of behavioural design and change management, which are concepts central to *Humology*.

14
Behavioural Design

'To uproot an old habit is sometimes a more painful thing, and vastly more difficult, than to wrench out a tooth.'
— Samuel Smiles, Scottish author and reformer (Smiles, 1856)

A re you familiar with behavioural economics, behavioural science and behavioural design? No longer the purview of academics and political advisors, in recent years these disciplines have entered mainstream business and are set to make an increasing impact. Despite the rising popularity of these areas, the distinction between the three can often create confusion. This chapter will explain these terms, the history behind this emerging philosophy, and how insights from these disciplines are entering the mainstream. Ultimately, it is context for understanding and appreciating the importance of behavioural design, which we feel is an essential skill for any technologist. Awareness and application of these bodies of knowledge are valuable tools that we hope you can add to your toolkit after reading *Humology*.

What is behavioural science?

Behavioural science is concerned with human behaviour, cultural anthropology, sociology and psychology. The focus of studies in this area includes the life and death of societal institutions, the evolution of communication and language in different eras and regions, and the forming and development of various types of relationships. We can consider behavioural science the overarching discipline from which behavioural economics has evolved. Be aware that the terminology is sometimes used loosely, and there can be an overlap between behavioural science and behavioural design.

Behavioural economics

Behavioural economics is the psychological study of people's decision-making process when making economic choices. That includes everything from what size of latte to order to investing for retirement. Rigorous testing is a fundamental component of behavioural economics, including field-testing new ideas.

Central to the development of behavioural economics was Richard Thaler and Cass Sunstein's premise that humans are not 'econs' or rational creatures from the pages of traditional economic textbooks who behave in perfectly logical ways that we now accept and understand to be far from reality (Thaler & Sunstein, 2008). Instead of weighing up options rationally, all too often humans rely on generalisations, biases and rules of thumb, and can behave in a myopic and impulsive manner.

Where is behavioural science used today?

Behavioural science has become an essential part of policymakers' toolkits. The World Bank and the United Nations now have dedicated teams of behavioural scientists who assist them in making people-centred policies that recognise the psychology of decision-making (United Nations, 2021).

The Behavioural Insights Team, also known as The Nudge Unit, is a social purpose company originally spun out of the UK government's Cabinet Office and now owned by innovation charity Nesta. Over a decade old, it has run more than 750 projects in the areas of healthcare, economic growth and humanitarian aid, and has been at the forefront of applying behavioural economics to real-world problems (Behavioural Insights Team, nd).

Deloitte has started to advocate using behavioural economics to reinvent HR practices since they are based on the best understanding of human psychology and that new ideas are rigorously tested, as per behavioural economics practices. We can see that this will significantly impact workplaces and open up new consulting opportunities and businesses (Guszcza, 2016).

Over thirteen years since Apple's first iPhone, consumers will queue up overnight to get their hands on the latest version. Despite what some might see as an expensive price tag, Apple has developed intense customer loyalty and dominates the smartphone market. How have they done this? Well, it is partially down to their clever use of behavioural economics. Some of the behavioural economics approaches they have adopted include:

- **The Endowment Effect:** This is the principle that you are more likely to value something you already own. Walk into any Apple store and you are allowed to test out the latest phones to your heart's content. You will soon start to feel like this is your phone and are more likely to feel comfortable with the price.

- **The Halo Effect:** This is a cognitive bias meaning we tend to make an overall impression of a person or product based on a single trait (eg he is handsome, therefore he must be trustworthy). Apple uses this bias to its advantage as each new product or version only adds to the perception of quality. There is a reason it is called the iPhone 12 and not some other clever name.

Of course, questionable application of behavioural economics can occur. Uber is reported to have experimented with 'video game techniques, graphics and non-cash rewards' that can nudge their drivers into working longer hours (Scheiber, 2017). They are also alleged to use a technique of alerting drivers that they are close to hitting a target when they attempt to log off (Scheiber, 2017).

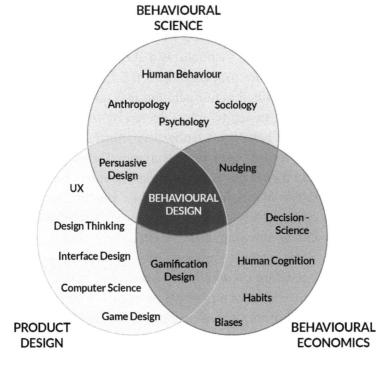

Figure 11 *Behavioural science*

Behavioural design

Behavioural design is a set of techniques and patterns you can use to change the way people behave and make decisions (Massey, 2016). We like to see it as bringing design principles together with behavioural economics. A behaviour is 'a habitual way of acting that is considered the norm or expectation' (Hull, 2017). Let's take a brief look at two of the most well-known approaches to behavioural design: the theory of planned behaviour (TPB) and the Fogg Behaviour Model.

The TPB is one of the most famous behavioural theories. It was developed by Icek Azjen in the 1980s and evolved from Fishbein and Azjen's Theory of Reasoned Action proposed in 1975 (Morris et al, 2012). TPB posits that our behaviour is influenced by our intention to act, which is driven by our attitude towards the behaviour, subjective norms and our perceived control over the behaviour (Morris et al, 2012). The theory has many use cases but has proved particularly successful in the public health area to help explain behaviours and actions associated with drug abuse, smoking and breastfeeding (LaMorte, 2019). Our attitude towards the behaviour may vary depending on whether we feel performing the behaviour will have a positive or negative outcome. Subjective norms also influence us; how do our peers or society in general view this behaviour? The final element is driven by how competent we feel in performing the behaviour.

In his 2020 book *Tiny Habits,* BJ Fogg introduced his behaviour model, which states that three critical elements need to be in place for a behaviour to occur at an exact moment. These are motivation, ability and a prompt (Fogg, 2020). We first need to have the motivation or desire to behave in a certain way or to perform a certain action. Here, we might want to understand the benefits of the behaviour or the WIIFM ('what's in it for me?'). Next, we must have the ability. BJ Fogg uses the example of Instagram, which was co-founded by Mike Krieger, a former student of Fogg at Stanford (Fogg, 2020). It takes as few as three clicks to post a photo on Instagram and, with the pervasiveness of smartphones, almost everyone can use Instagram. Finally, we have the all-important prompt or 'your cue to do the behaviour' (Fogg, 2020). This is equivalent to what Nir Eyal, author of *Hooked,* refers to as 'the spark plug in the engine' or the 'trigger' in his own Hooked model (Eyal, 2014).

When users are just starting to undertake a new action, external cues are vital. For example, if you intend to run every morning, placing your running shoes by your bed might be an effective cue. When it comes to creating effective product cues, we can place the product in the user's daily environment, use novel attention-grabbing cues, and build strong associations with existing routines. When we build new technology applications, often we ask users to change behaviours. Sometimes this is intentional and overt – Couch to 5K helps us build competence in running, Duolingo teaches us a new language, and Noom encourages us to form helpful eating habits.

We discuss our method of designing for behaviour change as part of the Humology Approach in Chapter 26. Whichever method you choose to help design your behaviours, we encourage you to focus on the 'critical few behaviours' as we can 'really only remember and change three to five key behaviours at one time' (Hull, 2017). Although referring specifically to designing behaviours for organisational cultural change, Hull's advice also applies to technology behaviours. She advises us to ensure these behaviours are 'tangible, repeatable, observable and measurable' (Hull, 2017).

Essentially, habits are a collection of learned behaviours built up through repetition. A deeper understanding of what drives those behaviours is critical when designing technology for human use. The key to changing behaviours is understanding the gap between a person's current behaviours, habits, preferences and schemas and the target behaviours that need to happen repeatedly for them to derive value from a product. Ultimately, behavioural change does not take place within the technology environment by itself – it is a human process and technologists must get to know the humans that will engage with their product or service.

Behavioural design is about helping others achieve their goals, not lining the pockets of shareholders. The chapters in Part 4 cover five critical human vulnerabilities that central to humankind – we are *impatient, impressionable, inattentive, irrational* and suffer from *inertia*. Looking at users – humans – in the context of these Five 'I's provides a framework from which to derive the insights needed to put humanity at the centre of the design process.

PART FOUR

Seeing Humans
Through Five 'I's

15
Impatient

'The gratification of one desire only makes way for another still more exacting.'
  — Timothy Shay Arthur, American novelist
    (Arthur, 1848)

We live in a culture of now. Have a question? Ask Google, Siri or Alexa and you'll have an answer in seconds. Eager to keep up with your favourite series? Stream it on-demand via Netflix, Apple TV or Amazon Prime. For everything else, Amazon can get it to you in 24 hours. Whatever we want can be found almost instantly online, so why shouldn't we expect instant results in other aspects of our lives? With an army of apps ready to cater to our every whim and an abundance of 'stuff' vying for our limited attention, it has never been easier to 'have it all'. We are the ultimate masters of convenience – turning our phones into our very own genie in a bottle experience. Just like Veruca Salt in the film *Willy Wonka and the Chocolate Factory*, we want it all and we want it now.[14]

While technology has greatly enabled a convenience-centric lifestyle, our desire for instant gratification is not a new phenomenon. Since the invention of the wheel, we have commandeered technology to produce more of what we want faster and cheaper. No company understands our need for speed more than Amazon. Not only does Amazon create temptation by offering us more than we could ever want, sooner than we expect, the company also has a relentless focus on removing any barriers that may prevent us from acting on impulse. Amazon's seamless '1-Click' checkout experience removed the annoying step of entering payment and delivery details for every purchase. In 2015, Amazon Dash was introduced – Wi-Fi enabled buttons in your home meant you could re-order washing powder while you were doing laundry, removing the need to store the information in your head for later. Alexa took over from Dash four years later – simply tell Alexa what you need and 'she' will look after the rest.

The result is myopic overconsumption – we have become hooked on instancy. Temptation fires up our

---

14 Veruca Salt is a spoilt, demanding child character in the 1971 film *Willy Wonka and the Chocolate Factory* (based on Roald Dahl's book, *Charlie and the Chocolate Factory*). Her famous tagline 'I want it now' led to an unfortunate ending.

impulse system, leaving our more rational system with the unenviable task of reasoning us back in the direction of our long-term goals. When barriers to consumption are removed, our willpower becomes the last line of defence. However, engaging willpower takes energy and conscious effort. With fast-paced lifestyles, constant distraction, and over-stimulation, we are less focused and more tired. In this state, our willpower is painfully exposed and vulnerable.

A bird in the hand

When making decisions, most of us are risk-averse. We are more likely to accept a small, but certain reward, over a larger gain that is less certain. This is partially because we have difficulty assessing and comprehending long-term consequences, but we also have an inherent bias that assigns a higher perceived value to today. Simply put, we value immediacy by default.

This concept, called hyperbolic discounting, is one of the most confounding findings of behavioural economics – we value smaller rewards sooner above larger rewards later. In an increasingly uncertain world, future rewards are discounted in our minds at an even greater rate, making instant rewards evermore salient. Hyperbolic discounting incentivises impulsivity and immediate gratification, making it difficult for us to prioritise our future selves. Hence, the everyday decisions we make can prioritise short-term gratification (like smoking, junk food, alcohol, drugs etc) at the expense of our long-term well-being.

The default mindset of 'spend now, save later' has frustrated the pensions and finance industries for years. Despite warnings that the planet is warming and water levels are rising, we continue as normal because we can't see and evaluate the future effectively. Many of the most serious and pervasive problems we face as individuals and as a society reflect the fact that we are temporally myopic creatures who are inherently incompetent at long-term planning.

The billion-dollar pleasure principle

If temptation isn't enough for us to grapple with, our brain chemistry is also conspiring to undermine our willpower. Each time we sense we're about to scratch an itch, the brain's pleasure centre releases a burst of dopamine, triggering feelings of happiness and satisfaction. The sensation is so pleasurable that we're left wanting more. Dubbed the behavioural cocaine of the tech world, dopamine is the secret ingredient behind the addictive nature of the 'like' button, notifications, the infinite scroll and autoplay functionality – features that are designed to seduce us into spending more time on apps than we intended. How addictive we find them depends on how often we feel the need to reach for a hit of dopamine to soothe a 'real-life' discomfort. The ongoing battle between dopamine and willpower shows just how strong the emotional brain is – rational thought is easily overpowered by the desires of the pleasure centre.

Our impulsivity has fuelled the meteoric growth of the social media industry, igniting fierce competition to keep eyes on screens. The profit equation is simple – increased time and attention from users results in greater revenue from advertisers. Inventor of the infinite scroll, and more recently an advocate for human-first design principles, Aza Raskin describes how profit influences technology design: 'to get your stock price up, the amount of time that people spend on your app has to go up. So, when you put that much pressure on that one number, you're going to start trying to invent new ways of getting people to stay hooked' (Panorama, 2018).

In *Hooked*, author Nir Eyal outlines the casino-like techniques being used within technology to build compulsive habits (Eyal, 2014). Regular feedback with a healthy dollop of variability gives us that Vegas rush. Like pulling a lever on a slot machine, we refresh our feeds to see what reward we get. The similarities don't end there – Vegas is carefully designed to maximise 'time on device', encourage us to lose track of time and hook the pleasure centre with a series of dopamine loops. With time-in-app now the default proxy for profitability in the social media industry, it's no surprise that the world's most successful technology companies are finding increasingly inventive ways to exploit our fallibilities.

Keen to replicate the success of these tactics, more companies are embracing design psychology. Borrowing heavily from the infinite scroll, Netflix's autoplay feature turns a seven-episode run of *Tiger King* into an unplanned six-hour marathon. As one episode closes, the next is conveniently queued up with a seamless transition. With a simple tweak that appeals to our impatient nature, Netflix shifts the user effort from making a conscious choice to watch an episode to choosing *not* to watch it. And like social media, Netflix measures success in terms of hours watched. As Netflix CEO Reed Hastings put it himself, 'The real measurement will be time – how do consumers vote with their evenings?' (New York Times Events, 2019).

The trouble with mindlessness

Today's users of technology have an appetite for immediate gratification and high expectations. Technology start-ups are responding with a completely frictionless first-time user experience. The practice of offering free trial periods in exchange for signing up is being replaced by seamless free-forever models with no credit card required. Delivering value before capturing value is now a key driver in any growth-marketing strategy. Successful companies have a relentless focus on customer success at the earliest stage using time-to-value (TTV) as a key metric. The longer it takes a user to get value from your product, the less likely that user is to convert to a long-term customer. In other words, those who embrace practices that speed up TTV will beat those who don't.

In a culture of now, you don't have long to make a great first impression. Game designers know that beginner's luck is a powerful hook – when you know what your user wants from your product, make it as easy as possible for them to do it. If intuition alone won't get them there, provide starter templates that help users reach their 'aha moment' as quickly as possible. Impatient users also love instant feedback. If they encounter an error, help them identify it, resolve it and get back on course as quickly as possible. If they sail through the process smoothly, let them know how competent they are. A well-designed product builds on the user's existing knowledge base and delivers value in phases, satisfying our need to feel competent and accomplished. The most compelling experiences hook users with an immediate rush of value, then keep them coming back for more with little spikes of delight along the way, offering benefits to novices and veterans alike.

Beware though – impatience turns to frustration quickly when expectations are not met. Our compulsion to be productive makes us intolerant of idle waiting times. One study of Internet users found that a single rebuffering delay while watching an online video increased stress levels by 15% (Ericsson, 2016). To put that into perspective, participants in this study compared the stress response to that of watching a horror movie or solving a complex mathematical problem. If your product involves waiting for processes to complete or information to be retrieved, look for opportunities for users to stay productive during that time.

Raising the horizon

If willpower is finite and temptations continue to proliferate, how can we avoid the dystopian future for humanity depicted in movies like *The Matrix* or *Wall-E*? Thankfully we are as impressionable as we are impatient. Communication is key when impatience is working against our best interests. Framing theory suggests that how information is presented (the frame) may influence the choices we make about how to process that information. Simply being exposed to words like 'future', 'long-term' and 'self-control' makes us more likely to think of the future.

Picturing the 'future you' that might result from your short- or long-term decisions also helps connect today's actions with tomorrow's outcomes. Some useful framing techniques are:

- **Metaphor:** To frame a conceptual idea through comparison with something familiar.

- **Stories:** To frame a topic via vivid and memorable language.

- **Tradition:** Cultural traditions that infuse the mundane with significance.

- **Slogan, jargon, catchphrase:** Use a catchy phrase to make it more memorable and relatable. For example, DeBeers famously boosted falling diamond sales with the iconic tagline 'A diamond is forever'.

- **Contrast:** To describe an object in terms of what it is not.

- **Spin:** To present a concept in a way that conveys a value judgement (positive or negative) that might not be immediately apparent to create an inherent bias by definition.

When it comes to communication, brevity is the name of the game. While asynchronous communication has become increasingly important in our 24/7 online world, our impatience has only increased. We've even invented acronyms that normalise our annoyance. For example, TL;DR (too long; didn't read) eventually gave way to TL;DV (too long; didn't view) in 2021 when we shifted from email to video messaging.

When it comes to launching a new product, impatience can be a double-edged sword. If you're lucky enough to gain traction on Product Hunt or TikTok, it may be short-lived. While a buzzworthy launch creates a flurry of interest and excitement, especially for those who are attracted to shiny new solutions or early adopters who are always watching out for the next new thing, expect a good portion of users to get no further than the sign-up process. With high churn and lower engagement, this cohort should be segregated when reporting user metrics.

Focus on reducing friction and eliminating barriers to entry for your product. Keep it simple, keep it shiny and make sure people remember why they signed up to begin with. If you don't have an onboarding plan or you ignore your new sign-ups while you finish that roadmap they were so excited about during sign-up, your early adopters will eventually give up on you. Impatience makes us quick to forget our good intentions and easily distracted by a shiny new object.

16
Impressionable

'Example, whether it be good or bad, has a powerful influence.'
— George Washington, 1st US President
(Washington, 1780)

W e may like to think we are in control of our thoughts and our behaviours, but psychology, and increasingly technology, tell a different story. Think about how you decide where and what to eat, what to watch on TV or where to visit on holiday? Like most of us you might rely on friends and family for recommendations, or you might consult an online rating platform like TripAdvisor. In fact, 50% of Americans rely on recommendations from friends and family when choosing a restaurant and 83% say that a word-of-mouth recommendation from a friend or family member makes them more likely to purchase that product or service.

In a world where we are overwhelmed with choice, we regularly outsource our information filtering to people and tools we trust to narrow down our choices. Powered by the data we provide, tech-savvy corporate giants use powerful algorithms to deliver what we want, based on what we've liked before – the top news in our Twitter feeds, the top-ranked search on Google, the top-rated products on Amazon, the most-watched series on Netflix. But how do these algorithms decide what to show us? In general, algorithms are programmed to mimic human decision-making. So, let's take a look under the hood to understand what influences the choices and the decisions we make.

The mechanics of influence

In his 1984 book *Influence: The Psychology of Persuasion*, Harvard psychologist Dr Robert Cialdini introduced six categories of influence thought to be particularly effective in purchasing and consumption decisions (Cialdini, 1984). Each is governed by a psychological principle – reciprocity, consistency, social proof, liking, authority and scarcity. These principles operate just below our conscious thought, in the zone of automaticity, making them almost universally applicable to humanity as a whole:

- **Reciprocity:** The concept of 'you scratch my back, and I'll scratch yours' is an apparently hardwired and uniquely human construct. We feel obligated to return a favour, in case we might be considered selfish. Content marketing is one of the most popular reciprocity strategies today. Each time we enter our email address to download a copy of a report from a website or subscribe to a newsletter, we are engaged in reciprocal behaviour. In technology design, this is known as the 'give before you take' principle. Engaging the reciprocity principle works like an inverted loyalty programme – the reward comes first in the hope that the consumer will earn it. When you offer something for free, you are inviting the consumer to engage in a reciprocity dance. Many will feel indebted enough to share with a friend at least.

- **Consistency:** We like to be consistent with the things we have said and done in the past, so we tend to exhibit the same behaviours throughout our lives. A preference for consistency can trigger consumer inertia – hence why many consumers fail to switch utility suppliers even when cheaper options are available. Personalisation algorithms use the consistency principle to deliver us more of the same – from Netflix to TikTok to LinkedIn, these algorithms curate what we see based on what we've seen before.

- **Social proof:** We look to the behaviour of others, in particular our peers, as a mental shortcut. It helps us cut through the noise and narrow down a range of options to choose from. We are influenced more by people who matter to us than by any marketing or feature design you can dream up regardless of whether it's a testimonial, a product rating, a driver in the case of Uber or a celebrity endorsement.

- **Likeability:** We say 'yes' more easily to likeable people because we associate attractive and charismatic individuals with talent, honesty and intelligence. While building 'likeability' into a product may seem a little elusive, users need to feel at ease while using your product. Once we deem a person, or product, likeable, we tend to interpret everything they do or say in a more favourable light, and the opposite is also true.

- **Authority:** We believe people who we perceive to be part of a higher order in society. I bet you paid a little more attention to this section when you realised *Doctor* Cialdini was also a psychologist at the prestigious Harvard University. We readily outsource our research and initial opinion on products to those we believe to be credible, knowledgeable resources. Endorsements, seals of approval and industry awards and badges are all opportunities to associate products with credible affiliates.

- **Scarcity:** We assign a higher value to things when we perceive them as being less available. This is the fundamental principle of demand and supply economics – we want more of what we can't have. The advertising industry has perfected the art of capturing the attention of our FOMOsapien nature.[15] It is difficult to get through a day without encountering a few FOMO-driven nudges like '10 people have this product in their basket' and '24 hours to shop at 70% off'.

The power of free is more popular than ever, with almost every new technology tool offering a free trial or free account with limited features. Whether we are loss-averse to the point of irrationality or we simply can't say no to getting something for near-zero effort, we are more likely to try something new when we consider the exchange low risk. In reality, most 'free' products have some form of exchange. For example, many founders will offer a product for free to attract early adopters they can study in a live environment – looking for cues and behaviours to inform the product roadmap and usability. However, a significant downside to offering free accounts is the high number of inactive or abandoned user accounts.

---

15 FOMO – an acronym used to describe the fear of missing out.

The butterfly effect

Social media has amplified the impact of social proof, igniting a butterfly effect that can turn ripples into tsunamis within minutes. With the power to make or break the next big thing, influencer marketing has grown into a multibillion-dollar economy. Such is their sway over their followers that mega influencers like Kim Kardashian can command six-figure sums for a single post on Instagram and an eight-year-old boy earned over $60 million posting toy reviews on his YouTube channel. A single tweet from Tesla CEO Elon Musk can send the cryptocurrency market on a rollercoaster ride – solidifying his unusual position as crypto's biggest influencer.

Uberinfluencers like Cristiano Ronaldo, the most followed person on Instagram, have the power to destabilise even the most established brands. During a high-profile press conference in 2021, Ronaldo calmly removed two prominently placed bottles of Coca-Cola, sponsors of the European Championships, from the camera's view and replaced them with a bottle of water. His single-worded utterance 'agua' wiped $4 billion off the value of Coca-Cola in the next few hours of trading (Westwood, 2021).

While influencer advocacy is having its golden moment with established brands, many younger companies are building shareability into their product design. Products like Zoom, Calendly and DocuSign grow through existing users by design – a simple email link to join, schedule or sign creates another user by default. Others like Airtable, Notion and Trello offer referral programmes where users are rewarded when someone uses their link to access the product for the first time. The reward is often expressed in dollar terms, as a credit against additional services or an unlocked feature or upgrade.

Rise of community – from *me* to *we*

One of the most critical elements of building a successful business in today's world is fostering a productive, lasting relationship with your audience. In a world dominated by noise and distraction, how do you find your audience and keep them engaged? Communities give every indication of being the answer.

Clubhouse was the coolest and most exclusive invite-only 'club' of 2021. If you didn't have an invite, it made you wonder if you needed cooler, more influential friends. Clubhouse brought its A-game to app design, engaging key persuasion tactics to ensure everyone heard about the new kid on the block:

- **Reciprocity:** Once you received an invite, the immediate sense of relief and excitement ensured you felt compelled to share your allocation of invites with your network.

- **Social proof:** With the opportunity to drop into a room with Drake, Oprah and Elon Musk, the broad appeal was enormous. Where else could you drop in and listen to Kanye and Elon having a casual chat in the middle of a global lockdown?

- **Scarcity:** Did we mention it is an exclusive invite-only club? The hottest new club in town, and it's only on iOS? Each member had a small number of invites to share among friends. Clubhouse took FOMO to a whole new level.

Notably, an invite to Clubhouse didn't come from the company – it came in the form of a text message from a friend. Each member had only two invites and chose to share one with you – so it must be cool, and you must be a valuable friend. You also immediately trust Clubhouse because your friend clearly does too.

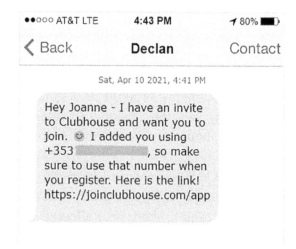

Figure 12 *Clubhouse invitation via text message*

With the continued sprawl of the Internet, it is easier to connect than ever before. However, the depth of those connections gets diluted as networks grow and multiply. Where feeds were once dominated by perfectly curated content, a growing desire for authentic human connection along with increased awareness of marketing nudges have given rise to a new era of digital interaction; one led by online communities like Reddit, Discord, Slack and Quora. Engagement with community sites has increased from 72% to 77% in the past two years, with over half of Internet users in the UK visiting online communities more than they were a few years ago. While 'we-centric' conversations are on the rise, there is a clear move away from 'me-centric' social sharing as the number of people sharing details of their personal life through traditional social media has declined by 35% over the past five years.

Trust in established media sources and media aggregators has also taken a blow. Social media once provided an outlet for people to be themselves, but by 2021 it was no longer a safe place for many. While people still want to express who they are online, they want to do it in a more meaningful, authentic and shared way. Our human need for connection hasn't changed – groups of people united by a common desire to be part of something bigger than themselves. This evolution led to Cialdini adding a seventh principle to his principles of influence in 2016. The 'Unity' principle refers to a sense of shared identity created between an influencer and the person being influenced. Shared language, ethnicity, location and beliefs all help to create a sense of kinship or oneness. However, feelings of togetherness can also be orchestrated when groups of people act together in unison towards a common goal or purpose. 'Put simply, *we* is the shared *me*.' (Cialdini, 2016).

Consider communities as a way to bring people together to share, co-create features and feel part of something bigger than themselves. Thoughtfully implemented, communities offer much more than belonging, they empower individuals to take action together that makes belonging matter.

17
Inattentive

'If you cut up a large diamond into little bits, it will
entirely lose the value it had as a whole. So a great
intellect sinks to the level of an ordinary one, as
soon as it is interrupted and disturbed.'
— Arthur Schopenhauer, German philosopher
(Schopenhauer, 1851)

In today's world, attention is a scarce resource, a
captive audience is a lucrative asset, and selling
eyeballs to the highest bidder is a profitable monetisation strategy. These are the basic principles of the
attention economy. In the attention economy, platforms aren't ever free, because, as the saying goes, if
you're not paying for the product, you *are* the product.
The corporate discovery that we're susceptible to our
attention being hacked has led to a fervent race fuelled

by technology and data – holding us captive to an endless parade of distractions from the moment we wake until we fall asleep.

The cost you won't see in accounts filed by Meta or TikTok is the erosion of our attention span – this cost is borne by humanity. In an age of distraction, constant interruptions are taking a toll on our ability to think, focus, solve problems and develop a human connection. In some business models, attention is the currency by which we pay for the service. For example, Spotify has two revenue streams: you can pay a subscription to listen ad-free, or pay with your attention and have your playlist regularly interrupted by ads.

Attention is a precious cognitive resource. All day, every day, we are bombarded with endless stimuli vying for our limited attention. Thankfully, our brains have a powerful filtering system that helps drown out unimportant inputs and shine a spotlight on what it deems worthy of our attention – this process is called selective attention. Selectively choosing what we pay attention to, such as listening attentively to a single conversation at a loud party, helps us tune out distractions and focus on what's important. As with any scarce resource, managing it carefully should be a priority.

When we succumb to distraction, we're motivated by a compulsion to relieve some discomfort in the present. There is a real concern that we are eroding our resilience and willpower by giving in to temptation so easily – the end result is the collective downgrading of humanity in which we no longer have the ability to stick with a complex task. As we re-surface after an hour inadvertently squandered on TikTok videos, we may regret that misspent time. However, the true cost is much greater. Because the attention economy is designed to prioritise compelling content above informative content, it systematically distorts our view of the world around us and leaves an indelible mark on society and humanity as a whole.

Algorithms designed to grab and hold our attention deliver infinite entertainment in a bid to keep us 'engaged'. However, constant interruptions and mindless scrolling are damaging our concentration, leaving us with fractured focus and an insatiable appetite for a hit of dopamine. We are nowhere and everywhere at once – a nation of information snackers scouring the Internet for our next hit. At work, many of us have become dependent on multitasking as a productivity hack, blind to the hidden longer-term cost of fragmented focus.

The attention budget

In Part 3, we learned that the brain's autopilot system functions as in-built protection against unnecessary spending from our finite attention budget. Automatic processes, such as habits and heuristics, act like shortcuts that preserve our attention and glucose levels – saving them for more complex tasks such as problem-solving and issue resolution. This form of automaticity is responsible for episodes of 'highway hypnosis' – when we arrive at a destination without recalling any distinctive landmarks along the way.

While the number of distractions vying for our attention increases daily, we have the same amount of mental processing power as we always have and the same number of minutes in a day. Our attentional system has a finite and depleting amount of energy available to it. As with our finances, we should invest our attentional funds responsibly. Consistent depletion of attention without adequate replenishment results in an overdraft – recognisable as mental fatigue or burnout. A depleted attentional budget also inhibits our ability to focus and make effective decisions.

We all have experience of trying to focus on a task while our thoughts are drifting elsewhere. The stimulus for staying on task comes from inside us (endogenous), while inputs from our environment (exogenous) tease our interest. Endogenous drivers of attention include intentions, habits and learned behaviours while exogenous drivers of attention refer to stimuli that capture our attention in our environment, such as colour, smell or sound. While attention merchants fight for a share of exogenous attention, we believe there is an urgent need for technologists to protect and support the endogenous capabilities that help us focus on the right things, in the right way, at the right time.

The cost of inattention

Lapses in attention happen regularly as we get side-tracked from our original intentions. We pick up our phone to make a call. Faced with a screen full of notifications, our endogenous attention is hijacked. Thirty minutes later, we're wondering why we picked up the phone in the first place. Attention lapses are common occurrences with real costs. Distracted drivers account for eight fatalities every day in the US (Covington, 2021), while distracted nurses were found to administer incorrect doses of medication 14% of the time and 75% of errors in laboratory processes were caused by unplanned interruptions (Kellogg et al, 2021).

When it comes to multitasking, we have bad news for those who believe in keeping many balls in the air at once: when we multitask, we actually aren't doing two things at once. Our brains are switching between each task concurrently and wasting precious attention and focus. Psychologists estimate we lose up to 20% of our productive time to context switching – and that percentage increases with the number of tasks we try to do at once. Switching between five competing tasks in a single hour adds a 'productivity tax' of 75% (Weinberg, 1992). Our brains are simply not designed to do two complex tasks at the same time. Sure, we can walk and talk at the same time, but try navigating your car into a tight parking spot while calculating 32% of 1,453.

Figure 13 below shows the time lost to context switching (trying to do two things at once) when faced with two tasks to complete. If we want to protect our focus and improve productivity, we need to stop starting and start finishing!

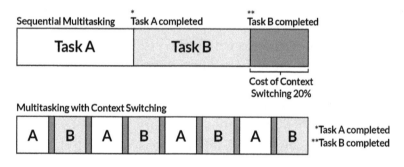

Figure 13 *The cost of multitasking*

Despite knowing that our attention span is dwindling, we can't seem to keep ourselves from switching focus. A recent study found proof of a neurological high whenever we switch to something new, which leaves us craving more (Yeykelis et al, 2014). Over time, switching becomes compulsive while silently eroding our ability to focus. It takes effort to stay on task. However, effort sounds like hard work – and hard work rarely gets done. Our human brains work best when we have a balance between flow (the type of deep focus where we lose track of time) and mind-lessness (allowing our focus to drift and wander).

The attention economists

A fractured attention span represents a significant challenge for every technologist. Anticipating where a user may need help and creating information that can capture the user's attention at that moment requires a deep understanding of how human attention works. In fact, managing selective attention is one of the key challenges for product designers. Sometimes referred to as inattentional blindness, when we focus on one thing we often fail to see what is hidden in plain sight. Great interfaces understand the limitations of human attention and design with that in mind.

One of the best-known experiments in this area is the 'invisible gorilla test' carried out by Christopher Chabris and Daniel Simons.[16] In this experiment, researchers asked participants to watch a video of people passing a basketball and asked them to count how many times the players wearing white passed the basketball. Afterwards, the participants were asked if they had noticed anything unusual while watching the video. About 50% of the participants reported see-ing nothing out of the ordinary. In reality, something very out of the ordinary had taken place – a person in

---

16   D Simons, Selective Attention Test, available at: www.youtube.com/ watch?v=vJG698U2Mvo (accessed 18 March 2022)

a gorilla suit strolled through the scene, turned to the camera, thumped their chest and walked away. If you haven't watched this experiment yet, it's certainly worth the time investment. When we are focused on a particular task, we fail to notice unexpected things in our visual field – the next time you log into an app or a piece of technology observe the use of space and information presented, and how it impacts your focus and attention.

Designing a product that feels effortless also poses a challenge when we need a user to pay attention to a task onscreen such as deleting a file or making irreversible changes to a document. When we are on autopilot, we often make choices based on muscle memory rather than intellectual calculation. Designed to appeal to the brain's salience network, technology often takes advantage of our inattention. Alerts and notifications, likes and comments, and variable rewards are all valid engagement techniques – it's the interruption and distraction they add to our daily lives that are contributing to our attention deficit.

Abundance – the enemy of attention

The Information Age has left us drowning in content – an information explosion as threatening as a population explosion. The increasing affordability and accessibility of technology are producing an abundant selection of products that address relatively similar needs. The proliferation of content can easily overwhelm the best of us – drinking from a firehose is not a sustainable way for humans to consume what technology has to offer.

We anticipate that the trends we now observe in designing for attention will continue to evolve over the next few years, as we adapt our selective attention skills to scroll past autoplaying videos and learn to ignore un-skippable ads. Many companies will continue to design habit-forming applications that entice users to spend a slice of their attention budget with them. Moreover, augmented reality and meta-verse players are already tooling up for the next war on attention, gambling on a future in which humans spend more time and attention inside a world that is designed to know us better than we know ourselves.

When we build new technologies, we design inter-faces and make decisions that demand a share of a user's attention. We believe every modern tech-nologist is also an attention economist, with a responsibility to use this scarce resource wisely and ensure its ongoing sustainability. In practice, this means creating technology solutions that do not unnecessarily deplete human attention and instead provide ample opportunities for replenishment.

18
Inert

'An object at rest stays at rest and an object in motion stays in motion with the same speed and in the same direction unless acted upon by an unbalanced force.'
— Sir Isaac Newton (Newton's first law of motion), British mathematician (Newton, 1687)

Inertia is one of the greatest riddles of human behaviour. Even though we know what's good for us, we choose comfort over effort almost without exception. Nutritional information and scientific guidance on health have never been more accessible and available. Why, then, do we continually make bad choices when it comes to food and exercise? Climate change is the defining crisis of our time, unfolding even more quickly than we feared, yet we fail to take immediate and necessary action. Instead, we suffer from something like paralysis. We give it various names: feeling 'stuck', 'unmotivated', 'apathetic' or by the more recently popular term, 'languishing'. With one foot on the accelerator and the other on the brake, we can't build enough momentum to propel us forward. Slowly, we sink back into the memory foam of our comfort zone and nothing changes. This is inertia.

During many of our corporate experiences driving and managing change, we met inertia in all cultures, high and low performers, engineers and accountants alike. Inertia is not like the typical resistance to change we have come to expect – it is something more confounding and frustrating. This gravitational pull towards the status quo acts as a diametrically opposing force to the need for agility and adaptability in a rapidly evolving world. Unaddressed, inertia poses a serious threat to the adoption of new technologies in the corporate world.

Playing for a draw

There are rival forces at play in everything we do – forces that push us forward (fuel) and forces that pull us back (friction). For a change in motion to occur, the sum of the forces must be greater than zero: that is, the fuel force must outweigh the friction force.

Let's imagine you intend to get to football training this evening after work. By 6pm, you're feeling tired but still determined as you navigate your way home in rush-hour traffic. At home, you realise your kit is still sitting in the laundry basket from last week. Not a problem; you pull on a tracksuit and peer outside. It's pouring rain – still not enough to dampen your spirits. A notification pops up on your phone – the team captain is stuck at work and won't make training this evening. Feeling the odds are against you this time, you decide to skip training, make dinner and get stuck into a good book. Two hours later, you've watched three episodes of *Squid Games* and your book remains untouched.

Sound familiar? We've all had moments when we feel like we're running to stand still. Despite our best efforts, we eventually tire out and give in to the forces pushing against us when we're not making progress. It starts with an intention (not to let work get in the way of exercise goals). Without any opposition, there's a high probability that we'll follow through. Minor obstacles (an unwashed kit and low energy levels) are not enough to dull our motivation. However, pouring rain and an absent captain tip the scales in favour of inaction. This is how best-laid plans are abandoned every day.

Users abandon products and services in the same way. A typical user starts the journey brimming with enthusiasm and muddles through until friction overwhelms the initial motivation and they 'churn' or give up trying. At this juncture, technologists may be tempted to push out more content, fresh instructions, attention-grabbing pop-ups or even layer on a digital adoption platform. However, adding more noise to a floundering user journey rarely increases adoption or engagement. The key to unlocking inertia lies in understanding the positive and negative forces impacting user behaviours. Armed with this knowledge, we can design strategies that add fuel, reduce friction and tip the scales in favour of action.

Momentum forces (fuel)

Ordinarily, we go to bed satisfied if we've accomplished something meaningful during the day. We may have closed out a large project, reached our step count or successfully negotiated a win-win solution to a tricky impasse at work. The sense of achievement makes us all feel good – we pursue it in big and small ways every day. From the moment we're born, we pursue mastery over ourselves and our environment, learning how things work by observing, exploring and manipulating them. We delight in the joy we feel when crawling gives way to walking, babbling to talking, and dependence to independence. This intrinsic desire to challenge ourselves purely to experience enjoyment from mastering something new is central to human motivation.

Self-Determination Theory (SDT) offers a framework for enhancing human motivation by focusing on satisfying three basic human needs:

- **Competence:** Our desire for progress and mastery of new situations and challenges

- **Autonomy:** Our desire to be in control of our actions and decisions

- **Relatedness:** Our need to have meaningful connections to others

Game designers and social psychologists have embraced SDT principles to boost engagement and emotional attachment with incredible results. From *Pokémon Go* to *Fortnite* and *Minecraft* to *Among Us*, viral gaming platforms embrace a self-directed, personalised approach to gaming. Coupled with endless permutations offering 'just right' challenges to every player and an estimated community of 2.7 billion gamers worldwide, online gaming provides an unprecedented opportunity to feel part of a unique tribe that is united in purpose.

Daniel Pink, the author of *Drive*, recognises purpose as another increasingly important motivational input (Pink, 2009). This can be a significant, transcendent purpose like climate change, or a 'small p' purpose like the daily wins we feel when we help a teammate solve a problem or resolve an issue for a customer. Once we've fanned the flames of motivation, what can we do to keep users engaged? The answer lies in finding a flow state. Famously described and investigated by Mihaly Csikszentmihalyi, flow is characterised by deep absorption during challenging activities to the point where we lose track of time (Csikszentmihalyi, 1990). Flow exists at the tipping point of frustration and boredom. Applying the Goldilocks principle, we need to determine the optimal challenge for a user taking into account their current abilities – the point where a user has enough competence and confidence to take on the challenge. When we experience flow, our engagement is high and we are intensely focused on the task. As we become more skilled, the degree of challenge also needs to rise to meet our newfound competence.

Building on SDT and the concept of flow, we propose the following conditions for an optimum user experience in a digital world:

- Clear expectations (what I need to do, how to do it)

- A runway of Goldilocks challenges (not too frustrating, not too boring)

- Self-directed exploration (allow for personalisation and meaningful choice)

- Immediate feedback (rewards for achievement, how well am I doing?)

- Distraction-free environment (maximum concentration, low cognitive load)

Technologists should keep in mind that motivation gives momentum to intention. Without intention, motivation will not result in action by itself. Instead, we will continue to grapple with inertia.

Resisting forces (friction)

At the root of inertia is the status quo bias. We are hard-wired to maintain the status quo by avoiding taking action. From this brief journey into the human psyche, you'll understand by now that we are all creatures of habit with a love of ease and comfort. We prefer to travel our neural superhighways at speed rather than digging new trenches with the promise of rewards too far in the future to make it worth it.

These behaviours show up in how we spend and save money, the food choices we make, and the way we binge-watch TV rather than exercise. But *why* do we prefer the status quo? Well, the answer is not that straightforward – scientists and psychologists have been fine-tuning research on this topic for hundreds of years.

The status quo bias has been attributed to a combination of loss aversion and the endowment effect. With loss aversion, when evaluating something new, we assign greater weight to potential losses than potential gains. With the endowment effect, we put a higher value on what we already own. If we have invested time and effort in creating the current reality, we are more determined to maintain it. These deeply ingrained psychological biases are universal, affecting every one of us. They are found wherever we resist changing our minds, beliefs, behaviours and habits.

To realistically consider something new, the benefit of making the change (the reward) needs to be *significantly* greater than the potential loss (the risk) for us to consider moving ahead. We value consistency because it promotes feelings of familiarity, safety and comfort. The discomfort we associate with change also drives our preference for linear newness rather than disruptive innovation. Consistency also breeds inertia in decision-making, making us more likely to repeat previous choices even where the outcomes have not been positive. The odds are naturally stacked against changing behaviours, even more so when behaviours become habits.

While it's a cliché to say that we can be workshy, there is undeniably some truth in it. Why is effort so terrifying? According to Carol Dweck, our reluctance to exert effort can be attributed to a belief that our natural abilities cannot be stretched (Dweck, 2007). We admire superheroes because they are gifted with supernatural abilities, not because they worked hard to cultivate those particular abilities. Great geniuses are not supposed to exert effort – effort is for those who don't have the ability, right? This 'nothing ventured, nothing lost' mindset links neatly with our bias for loss aversion – what if I exert the effort and fail miserably? Better not to take the chance.

If we consider this disposition for comfort, ease and the status quo as natural friction (similar to how a vehicle's tyres create traction when they meet the road surface), motivation is the force pressing on the gas, while an effortful user experience leans on the brakes. The role of the technologist is to craft the ultimate personalised driving experience.

19
Irrational

"'Contrariwise,' continued Tweedledee, 'if it was so, it might be; and if it were so, it would be; but as it isn't, it ain't. That's logic.'"
— Lewis Carroll, English author, *Through the Looking Glass* (Carroll, 1871)

While we like to think of ourselves as intellectual animals, we're far more instinctive and irrational than we tend to believe. Economists think of humans as 'econs' who, to quote Thaler and Sunstein, 'can think like Albert Einstein, store as much memory as IBM's Big Blue, and exercise the willpower of Mahatma Gandhi' (Thaler & Sunstein, 2008). In an economist's view, we're all well-informed, rational individuals who perform a ranked cost-benefit analysis before making decisions.

However, *real* people in the *real* world make mistakes, we self-sabotage, we say one thing and do another. We prioritise progress over perfection almost without fail because it's automatic, intuitive and effortless. In contrast, rationality takes energy and effort – neither of which we expend frivolously. The most significant influences on our decisions happen automatically; we're not even aware of the many instincts, biases and associations that impact our everyday choices. While there is no easy formula to understand irrational human behaviours, research provides some fascinating clues as to why we behave as we do.

Research shows that we are guided by a common set of principles and behaviours that appear to be pretty predictable. These patterns are so common that we consider them to be systematic – that is, we repeat them over and again. Magicians, mind-readers and even the advertising industry have tapped into these predictable patterns for centuries, but the recent explosion of rich behavioural data and powerful mining technologies has roused the interest of corporate giants. Decoding human behaviours is our modern-day gold prospecting – seduced by the potential size of the prize, the years of effortful mining are easily justified.

Irrational reactions

The very sniff of something being taken away from us can trigger psychological reactance. Think about the last time you were confronted by an unmanned hotel check-in desk, a self-service airport check-in, an automated customer service helpline or a chatbot? If you're like most humans, the shift from an 'at-your-service' focus to a 'help yourself' focus may trigger a range of emotions – an immediate sense of entitlement, followed by outrage, giving way to resigned frustration. When we react instinctively to a forced change, the perceived loss of control triggers resistance towards the change. Psychological reactance may not be logical – we may not even understand why we're so enraged – but we can't help feeling hard done by. A true rebel without a cause.

Irrational truths

Anyone who has even casually engaged with online dating apps, like *Bumble* or *Tinder*, has observed our penchant for self-enhancement. The lingo may be new, but the concepts are ageless – 'catfishing' (pretending to be someone else); 'kittenfishing' (shaving a few years off your age); and even 'hatfishing' (concealing a receding hairline under a hat) – new labels for the age-old concept of 'putting our best foot forward'. We don't set out to be deliberately dishonest, we're just hardwired to act in our own best interests. According to Dan Ariely, our tendency to engage in self-serving behaviour actually increases as we become more distant from the act, and when the medium of exchange is non-monetary (Ariely, 2008). These days, technology allows us to craft illusions of wealth and health online, with just enough moral distance to make it seem rational to ourselves. After all, if everyone else is doing it, it must be OK, right?

Information and ideas can also become increasingly believed and accepted as fact because of (a) repetition and (b) manipulation by interested parties. Timur Kuran and Cass Sunstein refer to the viral spread of information as an 'availability cascade' (Kuran & Sunstein, 1999). Essentially, the more an opinion is shared publicly, the more likely it is to be perceived as plausible. As Lenin is reputed to have said, 'if you make it trend, you make it true' (DiResta, 2018).

One of the easiest ways to gather feedback from a group of individuals is to use a survey or form. However, when it comes to asking people what they think, feel or would do, survey results are often misleading. Here's the challenge: when we're asked a rational question, we answer the way we think a rational person might do. Then we wander off and do something completely different. Experienced technologists know that if you want to understand users better, you don't ask what they would do – you have to observe them in the wild.

When faced with a complex problem that has no obvious or factual answer – such as the probability of an event, or how we feel about something – we substitute the original question with one we find easier to answer. The brain's System 1 is always trigger happy - eager to satisfice and move on. When you ask users questions, they may not answer the question you pose. In many cases, they'll answer a simple quick version of your question. This undermines some of the answers we get from surveys and it reminds us that we should not take responses too seriously when we ask people whether they will commit to changing their behaviour.

Irrational spending

When rational economics was drafted, we depended on cold hard cash as a currency. Cash allowed us to create a shared understanding of value. However, the near-universal presence of mobile devices coupled with the broad availability of digital wallet solutions and a global pandemic created the perfect recipe to accelerate the growth of non-cash transactions. The trend is significant as it disrupts our relationship with how we make monetary decisions. As we become more dependent on technology, we unravel the connective tissue between the decisions we make and the money we spend.

Money-related decisions go through a process called mental accounting to get to a decision. First, we split our pool of money into different categories, or mental accounts. Each has a unique purpose such as 'money to pay the bills', 'fun money' or 'money already committed'. When we consider an expenditure, our decision is greatly influenced by which mental account we are taking the funds from. An unexpected windfall is more likely to be spent on indulgent items – which may explain why so many lottery winners wind up bankrupt. This behaviour substantially undermines the principle of fungibility in traditional economics that states a dollar is still worth a dollar no matter how it is stored or what we spend it on.

An insight into how we make money decisions can influence how we charge for products. For example, when we pay for something in advance, we are almost compelled to consume it. The moment we pre-pay, we chalk up a deficit in our mental bank account. If we don't use the product we paid for, we're in the red. Being loss-averse by nature, we are duty-bound to turn that deficit into a profit. It's how we compute 'value for money' and rationalise an irrational purchase. It makes sense then to offer a discount to encourage users to commit to an annual plan. Annual plans are not only good for cash flow, they also work well for customer engagement. Users will seek out value for money merely to balance their fantasy bank account.

How do we determine what represents 'value for money'? Inputs from our environment are steering us more than you might think. For example, expensive price anchors can amplify the appearance of affordability and create an illusion of value for money. A price anchor is a focal point that we subconsciously compare to other available price points. If the focal point is high, everything else looks relatively more affordable. Similarly, if the focal price is low, we assess other price points as expensive.

However, no matter the payment terms or absolute price point, we will always choose the path of least effort when making purchasing decisions. Selecting from a small number of easy-to-understand pre-packaged purchasing options requires much less effort than asking a user to choose from a wide array of possible modules or add-ons. In general, pre-packaged bundles generate a higher uptake than a mix-and-match approach.

Irrational expectations

Have you noticed that we tend to overestimate the likelihood of good things happening to us, and underestimate bad ones? We fancy our chances of winning the lottery, yet underestimate our chances of being in a car accident, getting divorced or fighting cancer. Perhaps nowhere is unrealistic optimism more evident than in our estimation of the time needed to complete a task. Better known as the planning fallacy, we underestimate the time and resources needed to achieve our goals and overestimate our ability to deliver on time. Positive thinking is an evolutionary hallmark that helps us dream of possibilities, allowing us to be courageous and innovative. Without it, we would not have the resilience to keep pushing forward in the face of setbacks.

Context also matters. We don't know what we want until we see it in context. Whether we're shopping for a car or choosing a bottle of wine at a restaurant, context helps us focus on the comparative advantage of one choice over another. That's why we find three standard pricing options (or 'tiers') on most websites. Unsurprisingly, we also tend to gravitate towards the price in the middle, just like our good friend, Goldilocks.

We find it easier to compare apples with apples – not apples and oranges. This is why search engines and algorithms on everything from fashion websites to Amazon and Netflix provide us with 'personalised' lists of other similar things – helping us compare like with like. These comparisons act like a decoy to aid our decision-making. Their purpose is to offer us a choice that appears meaningful without distracting us from the decision at hand – and they often steer us one way or another. This is yet another example of the Goldilocks principle – when you know what too hot and too cold feel like, you will guide yourself towards the option that feels just right.

Technologists who understand that people are not entirely rational use behavioural design – the gap between what people say they want and what they do, or the gap between actual behaviours and intended behaviours. Behavioural design can be a powerful tool when building products that appeal to our emotional needs as well as our rational ones. By designing products based on how humans behave, we can ensure that they're intuitive and easy to use, and help them achieve their goals faster and easier. In other words, behavioural design is about making sure that technology works for us, instead of against us.

PART FIVE
Ethical Design

20
Have You Been Nudged?

'Those who can make you believe absurdities, can
make you commit atrocities.'
— Voltaire, French writer (Voltaire, 1785)

In his 2020 commencement speech, historian and
anthropologist Yuval Noah Harari described humans
as 'hackable animals' (Harari, 2020). While our digital footprints are being used today to predict human
choices and manipulate human desires, Harari predicts that further advances in biology, psychology and
technology mean we will soon have enough data to
reveal and predict how we feel. This fascination with
collecting data to understand and predict human
behaviour raises a pertinent question: how can we
ensure the ethical evolution of technology without
impeding progress?

We covered some of our brain's central limitations in the preceding chapters. We discussed that humans have a limited capacity to process the world around us. We spend the great majority of our time in autopilot mode; we are also guided by heuristics and biases impacting everything we do, think or say. We're emotional animals that won't conform to the mythical 'econs' creature dreamed up by economists. These limitations and our vulnerabilities are all part of what makes us human.

Why is any of this relevant to technologists? Because building technologies that deliver value to irrational humans requires thoughtful consideration of our limitations, thought patterns and behaviours. Technologists who understand what *actually* influences our decisions and behaviours, rather than relying on assumptions of how we *should* act will ultimately connect with humans on a deeper level. To influence humans to choose one technology over another, to ensure they can derive value, empower them to solve a pain point, and get them to pay attention to key moments or messages, you need to understand how we think and why we behave as we do.

Working with humans

Making decisions is hard – we don't have the time, energy or patience to thoroughly examine every decision we make. The more options we have, the more likely we will end up in cognitive paralysis. So, we resort to satisficing – making 'good enough' choices loaded with biases. However, we are easily influenced by how those choices are presented.

When we know that our decisions are influenced by the context in which they are made, we can optimise the environment to steer people towards the decision we would like them to make. In other words, when we know that choices are hard, we can use design to make decisions easier – this is the central tenet of choice architecture. The concept of nudging has become hugely popular as a form of choice architecture in recent years. Introduced in the seminal 2008 book *Nudge*, nudge theory aims to help us make better decisions that benefit us overall, using a subtle approach rather than mandates, penalties or regulation (Thaler & Sunstein, 2008). By preserving our freedom of choice, nudges minimise the resistance we feel when we're forced to comply with a new rule or policy. If we choose to ignore a nudge, there is no punishment – the ultimate choice is always ours.

When is a nudge not a nudge?

An effective nudge acts like a gentle hint – a reminder that a deadline is approaching, an alert to drink more water or an excited pet standing by the door eager to contribute to your step count. A nudge should never carry a financial incentive or penalty. Making unhealthy foods more expensive or charging a small amount for a plastic carrier bag go beyond a nudge. These measures fall under the umbrella of policy.

Unfortunately, there are many tactics that discourage us from doing the things we want to do or encourage us to take action which is not in our best interests. This is sludge, nudge's evil twin. Sludge tactics are rarely in the majority's best interests and often take advantage of our fallibility by steering our decisions in favour of the 'sludger'.[17] In his recent book on the topic, Cass Sunstein defines sludge in its broadest terms as a 'kind of transaction cost' that consists of 'frictions that separate people from what they want to get' (Sunstein, 2021).

When it comes to intent, sludge puts profit ahead of people. If we view a nudge as a form of persuasion, steering us in a particular direction but allowing us to go our own way, then sludge would be considered a manipulation – deliberately influencing someone else to our personal advantage, often without the other person's knowledge. We believe the biggest differentiator between a nudge and sludge is ethical intent. Consider the following table to be an informational nudge to guide decision-making around ethical nudging techniques.

17　While 'sludger' isn't (yet) a word, we'll use this term to refer to the entity designing and employing a nudge for the sole purpose of self-enrichment.

When a nudge is not a nudge

A nudge is...	A nudge is not...
Transparent and never misleading	An imperative like a mandate or a ban
Easy to opt out of	Attached to an economic incentive (or disincentive)
Designed to improve the welfare of the person being nudged	Win-lose – only the company wins
Win-win for the individual and company	

A nudge should promote...	A nudge should not promote...
Healthy behaviours	Unhealthy behaviours
Sensible spending	Overspending
Long-term well-being	Short-term gratification
Efficient use of resources	Overconsumption
Care for the planet	Harm to the planet
Contribution to society	Profit over people

Types of nudges

While no single taxonomy of nudges exists today, we encounter many different types of nudge every day. How choices are presented to us can significantly influence the decisions we make. One of the most prominent examples is in the use of defaults. Defaults save us from exerting any unnecessary effort and appeal to our herd mentality by signalling a social norm. Faced with a pre-selected default, we often assume that someone has done the research for us and trust that the default choice is in our best interests.

We can also influence decisions through presentation by adjusting the amount of effort needed to choose something. For example, we can adjust the effort needed to choose by putting chocolate out of reach or promoting one choice above another. We can highlight the consequences attached to each option presented – displaying nutritional information on a menu or calling attention to what's not covered under an insurance policy. We can also limit the number of options presented by bundling several options together or employing the decoy effect. You've likely come across the decoy effect if you've ever purchased a SaaS tool online. A third, less attractive option (the decoy) is presented to influence the perception of the other two choices and steer us towards a particular price.

When it comes to inertia, commitment devices act as an effective nudge to close the intention-action gap by reinforcing self-regulation. Text reminders (to take your medication, get some exercise or pay a bill on time) are also great tools for nudging us towards taking action.

In addition to physical nudges like the stop signs and traffic lights we're used to seeing on roads or crosswalks, there are also informational nudges – ways in which the information we need is presented to us to help us make better decisions. These may take the form of a warning label on a cigarette box or nutritional information on food packaging. These types of nudges aim to provide us with the right information in the right way at the right time, to help us make better or faster decisions. Because we have a limited attention budget and a restrictive bottleneck in our working memory, this type of nudge requires careful design to be effective.

Seeing humans through the Five 'I's framework can provide a helpful framework for designing an effective nudge.

Choice architecture with behavioural insights

Human fallibility	Characteristic	Nudge	Sludge
Impatient	We are impulsive	Defaults	Time-limited offers that never actually expire
	We prefer instant gratification	Real-time feedback	Pay-to-skip ads
		Progressive rewards	Fake FOMO nudges
	We value smaller rewards sooner over larger rewards later		Lengthy or complex cancellation procedures
Impressionable	We tend to follow the herd	Defaults can signal the most popular option	Celebrity endorsements for gambling apps
	We're influenced by authority and likeability	Highlighting how many similar people chose a particular option (social norms)	Notifications that promote impulsivity and scarcity
	We're motivated by scarcity		Proliferation of fake news
		Connecting action to impact	

Human fallibility	Characteristic	Nudge	Sludge
Irrational	We satisfice for convenience	Highlight the consequences of our choices	BOGO (buy one get one free) offers and other techniques designed to overcome willpower
	Emotions impact our choices	Limit choices	Use of decoy pricing – we gravitate towards the middle option
		Situating healthy foods more prominently than sugary snacks	Inciting hate, anger or violence
Inattentive	We don't read the small print	Cookie consent pop-ups as a reminder to be mindful of what we share	Malicious terms buried within lengthy T&Cs
	We're easily distracted	Confirmation before you delete a file	Automatic conversion of 'free' trials
	We often fail to see what is in plain sight	'Stay alert' nudges in self-driving cars	
Inert	We fail to follow through on our intentions	Text reminders (to drink more, stand, workout)	Rebates or warranties that require product registration by mail
	Given a choice, we are likely to choose the status quo	Commitment devices (step counters, goal trackers)	Long wait times for customer service
	We're loss-averse		

While every nudging mechanism is considered to be an effective behavioural intervention, many fail to offer cognitive efficiency during times when the brain has limited resources and/or has to make decisions under high time pressure. Researchers have found that defaults are consistently more effective in their ability to automatically change a person's behaviour than any other kind of nudge. The effectiveness of defaults may be due to our preference for cognitive ease – they act as mental short cuts, saving us energy we would otherwise use up thinking (Mertens et al, 2022).

A framework for ethical nudging

The sudden gold rush of behavioural data presents an enormous opportunity along with significant risks. The recommendation engines and personalisation algorithms used across social media, streaming services and music platforms nudge our choices daily. With the ability to hyper-personalise and micro-target, algorithmic nudging has mammoth potential to influence and mobilise small and large communities equally. Tomorrow's nudges will be even more adaptive – learning what works for us individually and evolving with us.

No one likes to think of themselves as a puppet on a string, yet when we examine our relationship with technology, there are plenty of examples where we have openly welcomed technology into our inner world. Seduced by convenience, we blindly accept cookies and use our social media accounts to sign

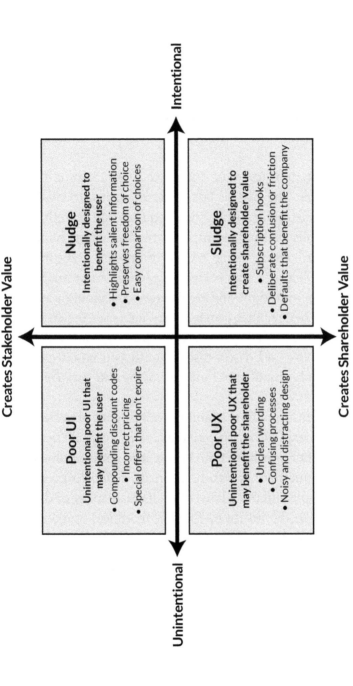

Figure 14 *Ethical nudge framework*

up for new services and apps, providing salient datapoints as we go. As we sleepwalk through technological threats, we inadvertently hand over a remote control of our behaviours. Can we complain when those buttons are pressed, our pleasure centre is activated and our thoughts are pre-programmed?

The potential for mass influence presents an ethical dilemma. The use of behavioural science to design and construct technologies requires strong ethical guardrails to prevent misuse. In the wrong hands, hyper-influence using AI has promoted radicalism and division in our societies. Algorithmic transparency is paramount and debiasing is becoming a new art. We believe that transparency increases the cost of hiding the truth. We recommend putting your nudges to the *New York Times* test – would you be happy if your nudge made the front page of the *New York Times*?

In the future, will this ability to influence at scale be used to exploit our impulsivity, or protect our dwindling attention to detail? Will it lead to technologies that manipulate for profit or incite action to protect our people and our planet? Will it create unity or division? Will the future be filled with ethical nudges or will we drown in sludge?

You decide.

21

The Hunter Becomes
The Hunted

'Without "ethical culture," there is no salvation for
humanity.'
— Albert Einstein (Einstein, 1951)

With the dawn of the new millennium came a
generation of interconnected devices and apps
that continually collect and exchange information with
other machines. Every day we use wearables, homes
tied to smart grids, self-driving vehicles and technology to regulate agriculture – there isn't a single part
of our lives that hasn't been touched by the sprawling
Internet of Things (IoT).

The benefits of having an Alexa device are compelling enough for us to swat away any brief concerns
we might have about our data. So what if Jeff Bezos

can see what we browse and buy on Amazon, what we watch on Prime, what we talk about in our homes, what we're reading on Kindle (or listening to on Audible) and even who rings the doorbell?[18] We're simply not *that* interesting and we have nothing to hide anyway, right? We've all had moments when we've rationalised away privacy concerns, clicked through a registration process without reading the T&Cs, and blindly dismissed those annoying cookie consent pop-ups for the umpteenth time.

While technology companies have always had access to our online activities, only recently have the tools become sophisticated enough to track, store and study our behaviours to guide us towards an outcome that is profitable for corporate giants. The aim of the EU's GDPR was to safeguard and protect the processing and sharing of personal data, and yet in 2021 60% of UK adults believed their smartphone was listening to them and using that information to display targeted ads (Nolsoe, 2021). With 75% of young adults reporting an oddly well-timed ad after speaking about a product with friends, it's no surprise that younger people are even more suspicious.

Even if we're unsure of the source, it's clear that our data is being used in ways we didn't anticipate. An investigation into the Ring doorbell app conducted by the Electronic Frontier Foundation 'found it to be

---

18 Amazon's Ring Video Doorbell has an embedded camera that connects to other devices such as your phone and computer.

packed with third-party trackers sending out a pleth-ora of customers' personally identifiable information' (Budington, 2020). Data aggregators depend on this process to build out comprehensive user profiles. The price we are paying for convenience is proving to be high.

Modern-day hunters trawl the Internet looking for easy prey – a passive, unthinking human seeking respite from decision overwhelm. The target is vul-nerable and easily lured by the promise of rewards. The predator's hunger is fuelled by the availability of rich surplus data – perfect ingredients for experi-mental algorithms. Their bloodlust is heightened by the thrill of uncovering further insights into human behaviour using a blend of machine learning and a team of behavioural scientists testing their predictive prowess. Vultures are circling from above, scavenging for leftovers. In the hunt for behavioural data, nothing is left behind.

In today's world, it is becoming increasingly difficult to tell fact from fiction. Traditional structures are not as effective as they once were and the concentration of wealth in Silicon Valley is defining a new form of power. We have created a technology-first world that harvests human experience to fuel growth engines and drive profits. On the journey, we have allowed technology to take the lead. How did we, the smartest species on earth, invent and empower our very own predator? How has the hunter become the hunted?

Unintended consequences

As humans, we tend to view the exponential through the eyes of linear and the unprecedented through the eyes of familiar. Seeing around corners or anticipating disruption do not come naturally to us. The chaos and uncertainty caused by an out-of-control virus have demonstrated that this trait is universally human. It is far more comfortable for us to view disruption as a temporary detour on the path to our pre-planned destination than as a permanent diversion.

When Zuckerberg and his fellow Harvard students toyed with a digital college face book in 2004, he could not have foreseen the journey that was about to unfold. He did not intentionally design a platform to be commandeered by political groups or to enable rampant misinformation. Yet, fuelled by the mantra of 'move fast and break things', the platform that hoped to 'give people the power to share and make the world more open and connected' also united groups of individuals with deviant ideals (Reagan, 2009). Time and again, Zuckerberg and his team struggled to balance their commitment to free expression with a rise in extremist behaviours and calls for violence. Before the 2016 presidential election, Facebook was viewed as a beacon of innovation and success in the US. However, the proliferation of fake news and rumours of Russian interference were the tipping point that triggered scrutiny from interested parties.

It's clear that the issues are complex and lack precedent – legislation often plays catch up with emerging social threats. It can take years to uncover, document and challenge unintended consequences. Meanwhile, the years in between are awash with pantomime and short-term fixes. Central to how we deal with these ongoing threats are the following questions: what is the responsibility of a technologist when a simple system (like a social sharing platform) interacts with more complex systems (like society, geopolitics and globalisation)? Should we accept the unintended consequences as a technological inevitability and press forward with innovation or should we chalk them up as a necessary cost of human progress on other fronts? Can we better anticipate and plan for these consequences?

Seeing around corners

Humans are simply terrible at predictions. We are so laden with bias and blind spots that an accurate prediction model would trigger cynicism more than celebration. Every financial forecast is flawed, exit polls are predictably inaccurate, and we second-guess even the most technical weather forecast. As Kahneman outlines in *Thinking, Fast and Slow*, all models of the future are wrong (Kahneman, 2012). Models, by their very nature, are simulations and therefore cannot possibly predict outcomes because of the complexity and volatility of the real world. A map of reality is not reality – even the best maps are imperfect approximations.

Until now, entrepreneurs have depended on a loose trade-off model when evaluating the potential impact their product may have on the world – betting that the benefits of technology, both anticipated and unintended, will outweigh the costs. However, this distinct lack of accountability enables entrepreneurs and their investors to dodge responsibility and complain about a lack of regulation. Why should they be held accountable for a harmful consequence they did not intend to create, particularly if their business has also generated some social good? As users and consumers of social media, we are familiar with the bystander effect when we witness online trolling but fail to take action. For a single constituent within a complex ecosystem, it's easy to stand back and assume someone else will figure it out. Perhaps we feel the regulators are more qualified for the job or we are waiting for someone to step forward and take ownership. In the meantime, there is a void of responsibility.

We're pretty good at simple, linear thinking – the type of thinking that fits into an 'if, then, else' formula. This type of first-order thinking is fast and easy. It happens when we look for something to solve an immediate problem without considering the consequences. Businesses fall into this short-termism trap as much as individuals. In our work, we often come across technology implementations that benefit one team while hurting another leading to an increase in work over-all. We also see start-ups struggling with systems that they have long outgrown. First-order thinking has some parallels with our autopilot mode of thinking, such as our willingness to jump to conclusions and our preference for instant gratification. This is espe-cially true if we are under pressure, overly confident in our abilities, experiencing strong emotions or mak-ing decisions in an echo chamber.

In contrast, second-order thinking is future-focused and more holistic. It requires us to not only con-sider our actions and their immediate consequences but the subsequent impact of those actions as well. Second-order thinking involves an understanding that, despite good intentions, interventions in com-plex systems often cause harm. We ask ourselves 'and then what?'. We understand that it's important to think through the consequences.

As an individual, you can cultivate second-order thinking using this simple six-point framework:

- **Be curious:** Consistently ask 'and then what?'.

- **Who benefits:** For every product decision, or feature request, ask who benefits? If not the user, then who?

- **Think long term:** Use the 10–10-10 technique. What do the consequences look like in 10 days, 10 months, 10 years?

- **Involve others:** Seek fresh perspectives to help shine a light on potential blind spots.

- **Perform a 'what if' analysis:** What happens if one or more of our key assumptions change? How sensitive are we to key changes in the external environment?

- **How will the ecosystem respond:** How might employees deal with this? How might competitors respond? Are suppliers impacted? How about regulators, or the planet?

22

The Dark Side
Of Influence

'Technology is a useful servant but a dangerous master.'
 — Christian Lange, Nobel Prize laureate
  (Branting, 1921)

According to Daniel Pink, we spend about 40% of our daily lives influencing others (Pink, 2012). That's twenty-four minutes of every waking hour persuading others to see our perspective, agree with our choices and endorse our ideas. We rely on our influencing skills every day to navigate the world and, in the main, we accept it as a normal part of human interaction. However, attempting to influence human behaviours at scale raises important questions about the ethics of mass persuasion. At the heart of the issue are the questions of what constitutes a better choice and who decides what is in our best interests?

What about using technology to not only influence but architect mass behaviour change? What level of influence is deemed acceptable? Do we trust technologists to have our best interests at heart? Intense pressure to achieve specific metrics or outcomes can encourage companies to overstep the boundaries of honest influence. With over five billion people accessing online sites and content in 2021, the potential to create harm on a global scale has never been more chilling (DOMO, 2021).

The algorithm of you

In the film *Her*, Joaquin Phoenix's character falls in love with his computer's virtual assistant, Samantha. Designed to adapt and evolve, Samantha can understand and respond to his thoughts and needs much better than other humans, including his long-term girlfriend and closest friends (Jonze, 2013). While the plot may seem dystopian, or even slightly comical at first, a recent study found that computer-based personality judgements are more accurate than those made by humans (Youyou et al, 2015). Comparing people's Facebook likes to their own answers in a personality questionnaire as well as the answers provided by their friends and family, the study found that Facebook outperformed any human, no matter their relation to the subjects. The results are pretty astounding:

- With just 10 likes, Facebook knows us better than our colleagues

- With 150 likes, Facebook knows more about us than our best friends or family

- With 250 likes, Facebook knows more about us than our parents

- With more than 300 likes, Facebook knows us better than our spouse does

If we can infer personality traits and predict behaviours with such a small data sample, we can only begin to imagine what is possible when we look at the expansive array of data being captured in our everyday lives. With technology having unprecedented access to our personal details, it's no wonder that many of us feel we are being hacked. Viewers of *The Social Dilemma* might recoil in horror as they learn how their own data is being used to shape our behaviours and shepherd us in droves towards the highest paying advertiser (Orlowski, 2020). The reality is, despite the ongoing decay in trust, both technologists and users continue to embrace Vegas-style design techniques and revenue models dependent on surveillance capitalism. We use freemium models as the gateway drug to lure new users before we roll out the hook: a sprinkling of behavioural cocaine.

Even though using technology isn't the same as using drugs or alcohol, the brain processes both addictions the same way. Whether we're playing video games, shopping online, creating TikToks or using a fitness tracker, a set of common design hooks sets out to erode our willpower, fragment our attention and feed our impulsivity. Getting a fix of dopamine from technology tricks our brain into thinking it no longer needs to create and release dopamine naturally, disrupting the brain's delicate chemical balance. Understanding how these business models interact with our human fallibilities allows us to defend ourselves and turn those vulnerabilities into strengths.

Weapons of mass manipulation

If you've ever struggled with a subscription that is almost impossible to quit or been surprised by add-ons at the checkout, you have unfortunately experienced first-hand some of the tricks employed when we put metrics above ethics. In the never-ending quest for more clicks, subscribers and sales, it's all too easy for technologists to fall prey to the lure of dark patterns. After all, winning hearts and minds is big business.

Dark patterns in technology refer to design choices that benefit the provider by coercing or deceiving us into making decisions that we might not have made if we were fully informed. At best, dark patterns are annoying and frustrating. At worst, they are misleading and deceptive – causing financial loss, privacy breaches and compulsive behaviours.[19] Each pattern is carefully crafted to exploit known fallibilities in human psychology. Using these patterns to drive revenue is not only unethical, it erodes trust.

The 2021 Edelman Trust Barometer indicates sweeping misinformation and wariness of institutions and leaders across the globe. With a swelling trust gap in relation to leaders in politics, business, the media and even religion, businesses are expected to focus on societal challenges with the same drive and resources they draw on to deliver profits (Edelman, 2021).

Unfortunately, many dark patterns are all too familiar to us – perceived scarcity to promote impulse buying, time-bound offers that are expiring soon, forced registration to access content. These patterns are so prevalent, we've become tolerant of and blind to their impact. Some of the most popular strategies used to exploit our known cognitive limitations or fallibilities are outlined in the following table.

---

19 British UX designer Harry Brignull maintains a fascinating 'Hall of Shame' on his website darkpatterns.org – if you're unsure what constitutes a dark pattern, we recommend a visit.

Popular dark patterns

Bait and switch	A user takes an action that indicates a desired outcome but ends up with a completely unforeseen outcome.
Forced continuity	A user signs up for a free trial using a credit card, but there is no opportunity to opt out once the trial has expired and no easy way to cancel.
Friend spam	An app asks for access to your contacts under the pretence of improving your enjoyment of the service. However, the intention is to spam your contacts to drive more sign-ups.
Hidden costs	Often a surprise at the end of a checkout process, these hidden costs may relate to taxes, insurance or delivery fees.
Roach motel	Possibly the most common dark pattern, the design makes it easy to sign up for a service but almost impossible to cancel.

Weapons of mass disinformation

In a world obsessed with content creation, our supply of information is contaminated by an overflow of superfluous content. Misinformation is everywhere and we are all vulnerable to it. However, the past decade has seen a worrying increase in the distribution of online propaganda – specifically *dis*information. While both misinformation and disinformation can be deceiving, disinformation is intentionally and maliciously misleading and motivated by economic gain.

Unregulated or unmoderated disinformation is of particular concern in countries such as Kenya, South Africa, Malaysia and the Philippines where social media are a main source of news (Watson, 2021). Reading news on social media is also fast becoming the norm for younger generations, making the propagation of fake news a raging infodemic waiting to happen.

Some of the most prominent examples of online disinformation campaigns related to the interference in the 2016 Brexit referendum and subsequently the 2016 US presidential election. Using techniques honed in military psychological operations (PSYOPS), outfits like Cambridge Analytica set out to replace truth with alternative narratives and virtual realities.

Leveraging the OCEAN psychological profiling model – openness, conscientiousness, extraversion, agreeableness and neuroticism – data scientist Chris Wylie experimented with a blend of social science and data science to predict voter behaviours and election outcomes. 'The goal in hacking', states Wylie, 'is to find a weak point in a system and then exploit that vulnerability. In psychological warfare, the weak points are flaws in how people think. If you're trying to hack a person's mind, you need to identify cognitive biases and then exploit them' (Wylie, 2019). This is, in essence, how data is weaponised: salient information is deliberately directed at an impressionable individual to affect emotions, beliefs and behaviours.

According to Wylie's (2019) account, the team at Cambridge Analytica was originally motivated by the enormous challenge and opportunity to create one giant societal simulation – like a real-life version of *The Sims*.[20] Teams of behavioural scientists, professors, researchers, academics, data scientists and anthropologists offered their insights and resources as the project took shape. To those interested in human behaviour, the chance to be involved in this game-changing project was not to be missed.

Working with Stephen Bannon, then the relatively unknown editor of the right-wing website *Breitbart News*, and armed with data from 87 million private Facebook accounts, the team at Cambridge Analytica launched a campaign aimed at their target audience. Based on psychological profiling, these targets were deemed more impulsive and more susceptible to conspiratorial thinking and, with the right kind of nudges, they could be lured into extreme thoughts or behaviour. Over short periods, the social media feeds of these individuals were bombarded with fake news and inflammatory content designed to manipulate at scale. Similar tactics were used to promote the Vote Leave campaign in the UK referendum on EU membership. With a lack of oversight from the platforms used to proliferate these campaigns, there was no

---

20 *The Sims* is a series of life simulation video games published by Electronic Arts. Players create virtual people called 'Sims', place them in homes, direct their moods and satisfy their desires.

safeguard in place to prevent bad actors from seeking to sow chaos (Wylie, 2019).

Inaction can also be considered action when the stakes are high. At the time of writing, Rohingya refugees from Myanmar are suing Meta Platforms (formerly Facebook, Inc) for $150 billion over allegations that the company failed to take appropriate action to moderate violent or dehumanising speech against ethnic minorities and enabled the spread of disinformation in a campaign of hate against the Rohingya people (NPR, 2021). While there are no accusations of Meta's involvement in actively promoting disinformation, the company is being repeatedly nudged to take responsibility for the unintended consequences of inactivity. Echoing the 2021 Edelman Trust report, we are looking to business leaders to be proactive on societal issues in collaboration with the partners in the ecosystem.

Throughout the global pandemic, we have also witnessed widespread disinformation about Covid-19 and its related vaccines. Rational questions around safety, efficacy and the long-term effects of a vaccine were often overshadowed by conspiracy theories. Claims were rife that the virus itself was a hoax and that the vaccine was a covert 5G surveillance implant or had been manufactured by Bill Gates for his own gain. Our propensity to believe in conspiracy theories can be a natural human reaction when the world around us appears chaotic. Our innate human desire to feel safe and secure can prompt our primitive brain to make complex and threatening situations more understandable and predictable. However, research findings show a strong correlation between distrust of government, belief in conspiracy theories, the frequency of using Twitter, and an unwillingness to get vaccinated (Jennings, 2021). Hence, the more disillusioned we become with the institutions we have leaned on for centuries, the more vulnerable we may be to ingesting disinformation.

Taken together, manipulation and disinformation not only represent a significant threat to democracy but a threat to humanity and society as we know it. Exploiting known human fallibilities for commercial gain is deeply unethical in itself. To deliberately set out to incite anger, hatred, violence and war is, we believe, morally bankrupt. In times of turbulence and volatility, trust is what holds society together – everyone has a part to play in restoring society and emerging from information bankruptcy.

23
From Egosystems To Ecosystems

'Today we must abandon competition and secure cooperation. This must be the central fact in all our considerations of international affairs; otherwise we face certain disaster.'
— Albert Einstein (Amrine, 1946)

When we change complex systems, we change the way the individual constituents in that system work. Wherever we have technology transformation, we also have societal transformation and, consequently, human transformation. In our increasingly connected world, new tools and products rarely exist in a vacuum – they exist within a larger ecosystem of businesses, stakeholders, users, political institutions and regulators. Advancements in technology are completely revamping the way society functions.

The advent of 5G and Web3 technologies, coupled with advances in biometrics, promise even more data, devices and interactions – heralding the era of hyperconnectivity. We expect this progress to drive displacement of labour markets by automation technologies that significantly reduce human labour. We anticipate a new age of disinformation challenges fuelled by deep fakes, while surveillance becomes normalised as technology makes it easier for Big Brother to watch over us. According to the Institute for the Future (IFTF), 'The hyperconnected world will be a sea change – forever altering how people work, play, learn, eat, shop, get around, get fit, stay healthy and entertain themselves and each other' (IFTF, 2020).

What challenges do we face in the twenty-first century? What changes will be required for us to continue to innovate at breakneck speeds while safeguarding our collective humanity? We need to move away from a growth-at-all-costs mentality towards an ecosystem mindset. No single company acting alone can unlock opportunity or excel in a hyperconnected future. Nor can we regulate the enormous power of AI systems at a national level. To succeed, we must think beyond cooperation towards mass collaboration.

Ethics above metrics

Growth metrics and targets have historically swayed product decisions and overruled internal objections in favour of pleasing investor expectations. When the value of a product is tied to engagement metrics, it is all too easy to lose sight of the human being impacted by a product. We know from experience that metrics have an outsized impact on internal decision-making.

Sarah Friar, CEO of Nextdoor, shares that, 'Some of the toughest discussions have been the trade-offs between engagement and growth versus slowing people down' (Hetzner, 2021).[21] One of the measures Nextdoor has taken to promote trust and prevent inflammatory content is to add a 'kindness reminder' that pops up when members are replying to posts. This courteous reminder of our humanity acts as a pre-emptive moderator. As Friar puts it, 'Why wait until after the fact? We actually put something right in front of you right while you're typing' (Hetzner, 2021).

While adding deliberate friction to the user experience challenges the unwritten rules of UX design, used effectively it can jolt us out of our unconscious thinking and encourage us to act with intent rather than habit. The impact is measurable – Nextdoor

---

21 https://nextdoor.com is a social networking service for neighbourhoods to share local knowledge and advice.

reports that over a third of people are more careful in how they word their replies. A similar method is used when a user is reporting a crime – checking for human bias and assumptions that may taint what is being reported. The results are startling, with instances of racial profiling reduced by 70% (Hetzner, 2021).

Do no harm

First articulated by economist Arthur Pigou in the 1920s, externalities are costs borne by society that go unaccounted for in the corporate world. Companies often ignore negative externalities because it makes them look more profitable or the impact will not be felt for many years. When externalities remain unaccounted for, social, health-related and environmental costs are borne by society while businesses report healthy profits. As we see with climate change, the individuals most impacted are often those with the least power to defend themselves.

Negative externalities may not be quantifiable in the same way as materials and labour, but they are costs to society – and a threat to humanity – just the same. In certain African countries, diamond production has been associated with terrorist funding, illegal smuggling and atrocious civil wars. The sector also contributes to significant air pollution, energy consumption and is known for poor working conditions. However, the dazzling array of rocks on display at any reputable jeweller will not reflect the hidden costs kept off the books by modern accounting rules.

Imagine, for a moment, including the costs of negative externalities in a standard business model – many of today's businesses would suddenly appear unviable. Organisations like True Price advocate for a more sustainable and holistic approach to pricing, while the UN is exploring true cost accounting to redefine the value of food.[22] A true price refers to the market price plus the unaccounted-for external costs. This provides a representation of the internal and external costs of the production of a product or service. True cost accounting advocates for the costs of positive and negative externalities to be included in management accounts. The idea is that companies will only be motivated to balance externalities to net positive when internal and external costs are accounted for.

While measuring externalities is undoubtedly a complex process, a simple ledger of externalities can immediately draw attention to significant imbalances in any business model. The aim is to ensure the pluses (+) more than outweigh the minuses (-).

---

22   https://trueprice.org

An indicative ledger of externalities

	Negative Externalities (−)	Positive Externalities (+)
Investors		Return on investment (ROI) +++
Users	Attention erosion −− Mental health −−− Polarisation −−− Privacy concerns −	Efficiency + Collaboration ++ Access to information ++ Freedom of speech ++
Employees	Burnout and stress − Bullying and harassment −−	Good working conditions + Self-actualisation + Job security + Diversity and inclusion +
Stakeholders	Political interference −−− Regulation −	Profits ++ Data and insights ++
Society	Information pollution − Addictive behaviours −− Social discord − Disinformation −	Data and insights + Innovation + Taxes +
Environment	Pollution − Energy consumption −	

Mercenary or missionary?

In the absence of a crystal ball, how can we take responsibility for how technology is used and abused once it is released into the world? How do we identify and track emerging risks? How do we consciously put in place product features, business models and values designed to protect our users, communities, society and companies from risk?

Embedding risk awareness in a company early on not only protects technologists and users from potential harms but also creates a more sustainable business model. In collaboration with the Omidyar Network, the IFTF has developed a useful toolkit to help technologists identify potential risks associated with how technologies could be used in the future. The Ethical OS toolkit is a great resource for all technologists at any stage of the journey.[23]

The curse of knowledge, not to mention our innate optimism bias, can make it more difficult to imagine a dystopian future for our creations. Engaging in a risk-spotting exercise is a great way to stretch our thinking or see outside ourselves. For example, take a hypothetical or emerging application of technology such as deep fake apps, biometrics, metaverse apps or neuralink technologies:

---

23 A copy of the toolkit, including the checklist mentioned, is available to download from https://ethicalos.org.

- Can you identify the potential risks to the ecosystem and its constituents?

- Looking at each application through the Five 'I's framework of human behaviour – impatience, impressionability, inattention, irrationality and inertia – does the technology support or exploit each of these human fallibilities?

- What designs and features could be introduced, or removed, to mitigate the risks identified and safeguard humanity?

Developing an instinctive awareness of the dangers of hotspots and blind spots ensures that technologists can make fast *and* informed decisions. The Ethical OS toolkit identifies eight risk zones in which hard-to-anticipate and unwelcome consequences are most likely to emerge. Being aware of how these risks show up in the 'real world' can help us connect cause and effect or identify design features that may unwittingly create risk exposure. If you are involved in product design decisions, we would recommend testing out the checklist on the Ethical OS website.

In the race to market, technology solutions are often developed with urgency while the societal impacts evolve over a much longer timeframe. In the rush to ship product and achieve deadlines, embracing foresight amid uncertainty can feel like unnecessary navel-gazing. However, we believe entrepreneurs and investors have the unique opportunity to set the tone when it comes to being a proactive, additive constituent in any ecosystem. To manage unintended consequences and address urgent threats to our collective welfare, we need practical and agile regulation. In the absence of this safeguard, active participation by a broad range of ecosystem constituents can collectively address emerging issues as they arise before any real harm is done.

We urge you to optimise for the whole, not just the individual. The tech world doesn't have to move fast and break things; we can move at a comfortable human pace, checking for blind spots as we go.

PART SIX
The Humology Approach

24
Know Your Purpose

'People don't buy WHAT you do; they buy WHY
you do it.'
—Simon Sinek

In his 2009 book *Start with Why* in which he implores
businesses, leaders and individuals to be authentic to be successful, Simon Sinek introduced us to his
Golden Circle model (Sinek, 2009). This model starts
with understanding, articulating and being true to
your purpose or, in other words, your 'why'. For technologists, this has never been more important. The
technologies we create and deploy reflect our personal values, beliefs and perspectives. In a borderless
digital world, purpose acts like a rudder as we navigate uncharted waters. As the rudder goes, so goes the

stern, and the boat turns. Purpose sets the direction and is the catalyst of sustainable forward momentum.

Recent years have seen the emergence of stakeholder capitalism. Klaus Schwab, founder of the World Economic Forum, was among the first to introduce this phrase about fifty years ago. Advocates of this approach believe that by moving from the current model of shareholder primacy to a model of stakeholder capitalism, we can build long-term value for everyone, which is 'increasingly good for the bottom line' (Hunt et al, 2021). This is achieved by considering the impact on all the stakeholders that a product or service touches, including employees, investors, customers and local communities. At the forefront of this movement is Paul Polman, former CEO of Unilever and co-founder of Imagine, a consultancy and foundation that helps companies to pursue the UN's sustainability goals. He has urged large corporations to look back to their roots to find their original broader purpose. He cites the example of his own experience working at Unilever, where he looked back to the company's foundation in the nineteenth century by Lord Lever and found that one of the company's original goals was shared prosperity and improved basic household hygiene in Victorian Britain (Hunt, 2021).

Organisations can verify that they are a force for good by being certified by B Lab, a non-profit organisation. Companies seek verification to show that they aim to balance purpose and profit and consider the impact of their business decisions on all stakeholders, including workers, customers, suppliers, community and the environment (B Lab, nd). Adopting a stakeholder capitalism mindset at the earliest stage can lead to authentic and long-term customer relationships. Aspiring to have a greater purpose and superior performance are not mutually exclusive. They reinforce each other and root businesses in healthy stakeholder ecosystems that can support real long-term economic growth

In *Start With Why*, Sinek (2009) cites several examples of leaders and organisations who illustrated the model's effectiveness, including JFK, Dr Martin Luther King Jr, Steve Jobs, Bill Gates, Apple and Southwest Airlines. Each was able to use the principles of the Golden Circle to achieve authenticity and make a significant impact on society.

There is a tremendous value for technologists in identifying your 'why' and applying the principles of the Golden Circle. This chapter will explain the model's relevance to your customers and employees and explain how you can apply it to your business.

The Golden Circle

Almost every organisation can articulate *what* they do, meaning the products or services they supply. The majority will also be able to tell you *how* they do what they do. However, Sinek suggests that few organisations can articulate *why* they do what they do – a secret ingredient for developing and maintaining authentic relationships with your customers and employees. From the outset, we should explain that your 'why' has to be broader than to make money. This can either be seen as a given or as a result of what you do, depending on your perspective.

When we think or communicate, our default mode is to start from the outside and move inward. We begin with the what and then explain the how; rarely do we even define the why. We see this when people discuss their new product or service or they discuss projects within organisations. Think how different your message, strategy or vision will be if you start at the circle's centre and move outwards – if you start with why.

Sinek compares his Golden Circle with a cross-section of the human brain. We have the limbic brain at the centre and the newest part of our brain, the neocortex, on the outside. The limbic brain is responsible for all of our emotions and feelings but has no capacity for language. When people resonate with our why, we are connecting to the limbic brain. Have you ever been asked to explain a purchase or a decision to engage with a vendor, and responded, 'well, it just felt right'? Who knew that gut feelings are taking place in our limbic brain?

To understand how the Golden Circle can be applied, let's consider how a hypothetical start-up, in this case, a low-code platform, might complete the circle to help them be clear about and articulate their why.

- **Why:** We are passionate about democratising access to low-code platforms to allow citizen developers and entrepreneurs to create technology tools and apps more easily, efficiently and quickly.

- **How:** Available on a low-cost subscription basis our unique selling proposition is our outstanding customer care and access to a community of like-minded users.

- **What:** We provide a low-code platform that is easy to use and navigate.

Being authentic

Unless you are the rare exception, your customers can probably buy your product or service from a competitor at a similar price, level of service and list of features. What can set you apart, especially when building long-term relationships, is authenticity. Authenticity in activating purpose means that what you 'do' aligns with what you 'say'.

If you're going to have a successful business, you need to attract, motivate and engage with an audience. If you can't do that, your business will probably never succeed, no matter how good your product or service is. One of the best ways to connect with your audience is through authenticity. So, what does it mean to be authentic in business? It means being more than just honest – it means being transparent about who you are and what you stand for. Being authentic will help cultivate lifelong relationships with your customers.

The opposite of being authentic is using manipulations, which can get you results but probably only in the short term. We have all seen examples of manipulations: price reductions, promotions, fear, peer pressure and aspirational messages. Of course, some level of influence is necessary. We all do it, to some extent, both in our business and personal lives. But we want you to be clear when, how and to what extent you use it, and also to be aware that manipulation may win business, even repeat business, but it won't breed loyalty.

Attracting talent

You also need to understand your why if you want to attract key talent to your company and retain it in today's competitive employment market. Talent increasingly wants to work with companies who share their values and beliefs. As your business expands, you will find that your employees have more dealings with your customers than you do. So, it is vital that they understand and can exhibit your why. Recruitment of your first few hires can be one of the most important decisions you make as a start-up. It can be a mistake to automatically chase the brightest, most determined and ambitious candidates. It would be best to give as much weight to whether they align with your values as to their technical abilities. Atlassian, the Australian-founded software giant, recently overhauled its performance management system to help it weed out 'brilliant jerks' from the company (Masige, 2019). These employees can be super-smart and deliver outstanding results, but they are oblivious to their negative impact on others and can make work a living hell for their co-workers.

A business leader's role is to steer the ship. You can't be everywhere at once, so you need to delegate tasks and employ strategies that will help you achieve your vision. Bill Gates had his Paul Allen and Steve Jobs had his Steve Wozniak. Whether they are co-founders or your first few critical hires, ensure you surround yourself with the right people. They can provide the how to your why. Be aware that they will have their own why as well; they are not just vessels or carriers of yours.

Purpose statement

The essence of a purpose statement is to ask why. Why are you in business? Why do you do what you do? Why this industry? Why are you using technology? You need to think about purpose deeply. Dig into it as much as you can.

Mission and vision statements are two terms that are often conflated or confused. A business mission statement is a concise description of your company's purpose. It's a set of principles that can help guide your business decisions and ensure that you're always working towards achieving the same goal. A vision statement, on the other hand, is something more aspirational. It's about where you want to be in five, ten or even twenty years – it paints a picture of what your future business will look like. While they may sound similar at first glance, some fundamental differences make them useful for different situations and types of companies.

A mission statement clarifies what the company wants to achieve, who they want to support and why they help them. A vision statement describes where the company wants a community, or the world, to be as a result of the company's services. Thus, a mission statement is a roadmap for the company's vision statement.

A vision statement is a more detailed statement. It includes everything your company does – from the workers you hire to your products and services – and explains what makes your business unique. Here are some examples (O'Donovan, 2020) of vision statements to inspire you:

- **Microsoft:** 'Empower every person and every organisation on the planet to achieve more.'

- **Heinz:** 'Our VISION, quite simply, is to be: "The World's Premier Food Company, Offering Nutritious, Superior Tasting Foods to People Everywhere".'

- **Nike:** 'Bring inspiration and innovation to every athlete* in the world. (*If you have a body, you are an athlete.)'

Once we have put the rudder in place, it's time to set a destination. What problems does my product solve? Why should someone buy my product?

25
What Problem Are You Trying To Solve?

'People don't want to buy a quarter-inch drill. They want a quarter-inch hole!'
— Theodore Levitt (Ulwick, 2016)

The 'Jobs-to-be-Done' framework – you've probably heard of it, but you might not know how it applies specifically to your business. In this chapter, we will explain the framework so you can apply it to your business or project. Central to the framework is the notion that people do not simply buy a product or a service – they 'hire' a product or a service to get a job done. Focusing on what your customer is trying to accomplish helps you understand what they might hire to help them achieve it quicker or better and why. This then informs the products or services you develop and how you market and sell them.

The creation of the Jobs-to-be-Done (JTBD) framework is credited to Anthony Ulwick and Clayton Christensen, who have refined and iterated the process over the past thirty years. Ulwick was inspired to create the framework after being involved in the PCjr flop at IBM in the 1980s, which cost IBM over a billion dollars. We looked to Ulwick's book *Jobs To Be Done: Theory to Practice* (Ulwick, 2016) as inspiration for this chapter.

We feel the JTBD framework is a novel approach to innovating and understanding why a customer would want to use your product that allows a business to capture, organise, categorise and prioritise customer needs. It is especially beneficial for technologists. It will allow you to truly understand your customers' needs (and which of those are not being appropriately addressed) and allow you to focus your product or service on meeting these needs. A study by pricing firm Simon-Kucher & Partners showed that 72% of all new product introductions failed to live up to expectations. That seems like quite a poor success rate, we are sure you will agree.

In the previous chapter, we looked at the 'why' from the Golden Circle – you can consider the JTBD as your 'what'. A central tenet of the JTBD framework is that customers hire solutions to get jobs done. It is crucial to be clear on the exact product or service you provide but, more importantly, to ensure that you are addressing true customer needs and not just offering a solution you feel a customer should or could use.

The traditional approach to innovation and identifying customer needs used by many organisations, including start-ups, is an ideas-first method. You may have been involved in ideation or brainstorming sessions that resulted in hundreds of post-it notes being stuck on a wall in your office. This approach aims to generate as many ideas as possible and quickly filter out those unlikely to succeed. This is the 'test fast, fail fast' approach advocated by business guru Tom Peters in *Thriving on Chaos* (Peters, 1987). It relies more on luck and intuition than a structured scientific process. The JTBD framework provides an alternate method.

The JTBD framework

The central part of the JTBD framework is the core functional job, which is the job the end-user is trying to do. This should be contained within a single statement and have three main attributes: it should be solution-agnostic, apply across geographical boundaries and be stable (ie not change considerably over time). A job statement begins with a verb and is followed by a noun. The statement should also include a contextual clarifier. We have included some examples in the following table to illustrate this concept. Note the core functional job is not 'listen to music while on the go using Spotify'.

Real-life core functional job examples

Core functional job	Examples of related product/service
Travel from A to B in comfort	Uber or taxi
Cut a piece of wood in a straight line	Electric saw
Book a holiday online	Trivago or Trip Advisor
Listen to music while on the go	Spotify
Watch a movie at home	Netflix or iTunes
Purchase an item online	Credit or debit card
Study a subject online	Coursera or Udemy
Manage my recruitment process digitally	Talent management system or applicant tracking system (ATS)

We can then turn our attention to the most critical component of the JTBD framework: generating our desired outcome statements. These are metrics used by your customers to measure success and value as they perform the core functional job. There could be dozens of these associated with a core functional job, but we feel that if you, as a start-up, can articulate ten or more you are off to a good start.

Much like the core functional job statements, the desired outcome statements have a particular format and should contain:

- A direction of improvement

- A metric

- An object of control

- A contextual clarifier

Here are two examples to help illustrate the format/ concept:

- Minimise the time it takes to fill a vacancy for key positions

- Minimise the time it takes for my transport to arrive

It can be helpful to consider any other related jobs your customer is trying to do. For start-ups, this can lead to insights into potential opportunities to evolve your service or product into a platform that serves multiple related job needs. To understand and relate to your customers, also consider the customer's emotional and social jobs; for example, the customer may want to feel appreciated by their peers or be seen as being socially responsible in the community. Considerable insight can also be gained by understanding the emotional jobs that are important to your customer to get the core functional jobs done.

After a product has been sold, several people in an organisation will be responsible for installing, maintaining and supporting it. Understanding these consumption chain jobs and making life easier for the stakeholders involved can help your sales process and make managing these accounts much easier. A simple example for a tech product is your client's IT function, which may be tasked with providing level one (help-desk) support for your product.

Don't forget to consider the financial outcomes that your client's organisation is trying to achieve. For our 'cut a piece of wood in a straight line' core functional job in the table above, the CFO of the building company may want to reduce time wasted on re-work. The buyer of our ATS may wish to reduce lost sales revenue by decreasing the time it takes to hire new sales associates. It is worth noting the recent trend for organisations' buying decisions to come from the bottom up instead of the traditional top-down approach.

Now that you have all these outcomes, you can look at your customer segments, remembering that 'success in any market comes by helping customers get a job done better and/or more cheaply' (Ulwick, 2016). We can categorise customers into three buckets: those whose needs are underserved, those whose needs are overserved and those whose needs are being adequately addressed. To determine this, Ulwick uses an 'opportunity landscape' whereby desired outcomes for competing offerings are plotted on a satisfaction versus importance grid (Ulwick, 2016). Note that by overserved, we mean customers who pay for features that they don't need; for example, a small enterprise using an ERP system more suitable for a larger organisation (eg Workday, SAP, etc).

Growth strategy

Armed with these new insights into your customers and their needs, you can determine your growth strategy. Review the products the customer is currently hiring to get their job done and decide if you will do it better or cheaper. As a technologist, you can either provide products or services that are:

- Better and more expensive – a differentiated strategy

- Better and less expensive – a dominant strategy

- Worse and less expensive – a disruptive strategy

- Worse and more expensive – a discrete strategy

These four strategies are illustrated below.

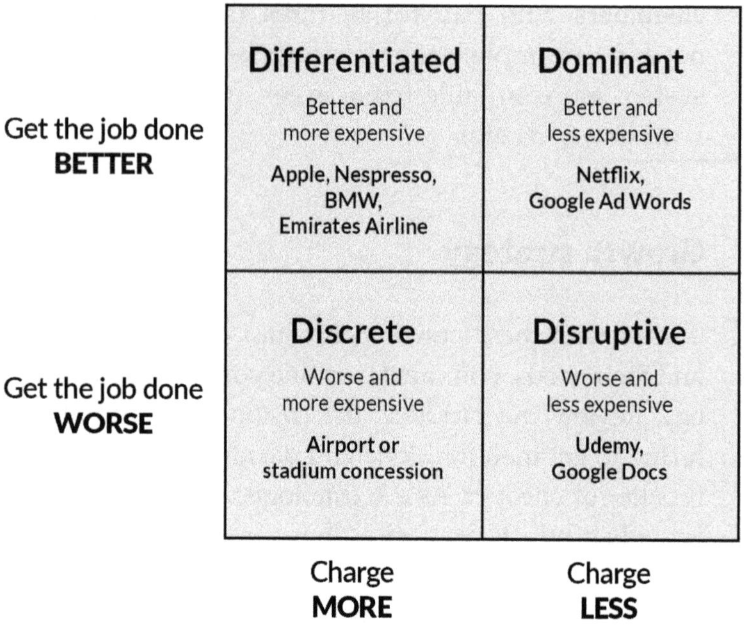

Get the job done **BETTER**	**Differentiated** Better and more expensive Apple, Nespresso, BMW, Emirates Airline	**Dominant** Better and less expensive Netflix, Google Ad Words
Get the job done **WORSE**	**Discrete** Worse and more expensive Airport or stadium concession	**Disruptive** Worse and less expensive Udemy, Google Docs
	Charge **MORE**	Charge **LESS**

Figure 15 *JTBD growth strategies (Ulwick, 2016)*

26
Humology

'The best time to plant a tree is twenty years ago.
The second-best time is today.'
— Chinese proverb

Recent developments in frontier technologies hold the promise of a brighter future, from climate action and health to more democratic and inclusive communities. Yet, left unchecked, technology also has the power to create global challenges and crises – intentionally or as a byproduct. Emerging technologies are open to interpretation; they are not deterministic. We can choose to harness their potential for the common good, leaving no human behind. We must do so.

The *Humology* design framework acts as a guide to the thoughtful and considered design and implementation of technology. Our extensive combined professional experience coupled with dedicated research have been synthesised into a practical, easy-to-use framework for all technologists. It unites the work of researchers, designers, engineers, policymakers and technologists to steer technological innovation towards the protection and improvement of humanity and the world we live in.

The framework is centred around the belief that the relationship between humans and technology is interdependent and symbiotic. Specifically, we advocate for the consideration of inherent human fallibility and the human cost of disruptive change systematically throughout the product design process. Our goal is to protect and strengthen humanity while causing minimal damage or disruption to the ecosystems we inhabit. In developing the framework, we have drawn inspiration from psychology, behavioural science, psychology, anthropology and change management, among other disciplines.

While we are aware there is considerable debate at every level around moral and ethical frameworks and significant ongoing research into human behaviours, we aim to provide a practical and helpful framework. In doing so, we have adopted models aimed at progressing beyond debate and discussion. We do not claim that our method is foolproof or better than others, but we believe that action is needed now to correct the imbalance that has emerged in our relationship with technology. Sometimes, actions speak louder than words.

We believe any technologist can adopt the tools and techniques independent of a product's maturity. It is never too late to embrace Humology.

Know your purpose – why do you do what you do?

Finding purpose is like peeling away the layers of an onion until you get to the inner core. At the centre, you discover the inspiration that drives you forward. Purpose offers a new lens through which to view the world and a filter to make better decisions. To uncover your purpose, begin by documenting the defining moments of your professional life to date, then search for connections and common threads. As the process unfolds, key themes will emerge that resonate with your sense of identity. Think of how these themes would look on a billboard – in ten words or less, what would they say about you?

Keep iterating until you hit on a motto that resonates completely. Give it the tattoo test – would you be proud to have this motto immortalised in indelible ink? Once you have settled on your purpose, put it to work:

1. Use the Golden Circle approach outlined in Chapter 24 to help articulate your purpose statement or your 'why'.

2. Incorporate your purpose into mission and/or vision statements for your product.

3. Imbue your teams with purpose – let it radiate out from the core and penetrate all aspects of your business.

4. Use your purpose statement as a litmus test when navigating business and product decisions.

As an example, your purpose statement might look like this:

> To support the prosperity of our planet and everyone who lives here so that every human can be fulfilled.

Understand the problem

What do you want to accomplish? What will be different about the world when your product is launched? Successful products are created when they meet an unmet need. When you're trying to solve a problem, it's easy to get caught up in the details of your product and lose sight of what your customers really need.

By understanding what a user might look to achieve using your product, you gain a better understanding of that person's needs and motivations. Armed with purpose as your guide, let's look at the steps to craft a solid job statement:

1. **Document the core functional job(s) that your user is trying to achieve.** A job statement should begin with a verb and follow with a noun. The statement should also include a contextual clarifier.

   Think: 'Action + Object + Context'.

   Core functional job statement

Action	Object	Context
Manage	the recruitment process	digitally

2. **Generate the desired outcome statements.** Think about the criteria someone might use when deciding which product to use. Outcome statements provide insight into how a user might measure value. Effective statements contain a direction of improvement, a metric, an object of control and a contextual clarifier.

   Think: 'Improvement + Measure + Object of Control'

   The measure hints at how the customer will measure value – typically in terms of time, predictability and efficiency, which can be used to form your core product metrics.

Desired outcome(s) statement

Improvement	Measure	Object of Control
Minimise	the time spent	doing administration
Minimise	the effort involved in	preparing reports
Increase	the number of candidates for	each open position
Minimise	the time it takes to	hire a candidate

While every product will have multiple goals, a single clear outcome helps to gauge success and measure value creation. In the example shown in the table above, focusing on the first outcome statement could free up time to meet the other outcome statements.

3. **Choose your growth strategy.** Will it be differentiated (*better and more expensive*), dominant (*better and less expensive*), disruptive (*worse and less expensive*) or discrete (*worse and more expensive*). Refer to the JTBD framework in Chapter 25.

Prioritise the human experience – target behaviours

Having identified the highest priority outcome to be derived from the product, we need to translate that into user actions – a list of specific behaviours that a user might perform to realise the desired outcome. Actions should have a direct and clear link to the outcome. Keep searching until you identify three to five key actions that users would need to do *repeatedly* to reach the desired outcomes. Repeated actions are defined as behaviours.

Behaviours should always be observable, actual and measurable actions that users will take. Feelings and thoughts are relevant in so far as they drive behaviours. At this stage, we're not concerned with *how* the product will drive these behaviours, only that certain behaviours are key to achieving the desired outcomes.

Here are some prompts to get you thinking along the right lines:

- What is currently stopping the user from achieving the desired outcome?

- If you have identified competitor products, what doesn't work well for their users? Why?

- Use our Five 'I's framework – how might impatience, impressionability, inattention, irrationality and inertia drive actions and behaviours?

If you are feeling stuck, practice by generating key target behaviours that underpin a product that you are familiar with.

By now, we are beginning to build up an idea for a product that fits into our vision:

From why to what

Purpose	To support the prosperity of our planet and everyone who lives here so that every human can be fulfilled
Vision	To be the leader in matching talent with opportunity in the communities we serve
Core functional job	To manage the recruitment process digitally
Desired outcome(s)	To minimise the time spent managing the process
Target behaviours	Users conduct all parts of the hiring process digitally
	Users invite candidates to engage in the digital process
	Users actively manage the process from start to end

Prioritise the human experience – mapping existing behaviours

Who will be using and interacting with your product? Let's get curious about how these humans currently think and act. Using our Five 'I's framework, identify the current beliefs (*what we think*) and behaviours (*how we act*) that are likely to affect your target users.

For example, looking at users through an *impatience* lens might surface an underlying belief that every-thing in that person's job is a high priority. This belief might show up as frustration with learning a

Identifying human behaviours through the Five 'I's framework

	Behavioural drivers	Underlying belief	Resulting behaviours
Impatience	We are prone to impulsivity We prefer instant gratification We value smaller rewards sooner over larger ones later We find it hard to value our future selves	Eg Everything is urgent and high priority	Will not invest time in learning a new tool
Impressionability	We like to be consistent and follow social norms We are wired for reciprocity We're influenced by likeability and authority figures We act on scarcity	Eg It's above my pay grade to have an opinion	Will only embrace something new when other (important) people do
Inattention	We have a limited attention budget We are impulsive and prone to distractibility We often miss what is hidden in plain sight We cannot effectively multitask	Eg I am more productive when juggling lots of things to do	Limited attention span to focus on a singular task
Irrationality	We are predictably irrational We are driven by emotions and gut feeling We place different subjective values on money We say one thing and do another We are loss-averse by nature – losses loom larger than gains	Eg I want to be fit, but it's such hard work	Good intentions easily give way to the status quo
Inertia	We prefer the status quo We're motivated by progress and self-improvement We value autonomy	Eg I think my Excel spreadsheet is really cool	Resists changing to a new system

new system or bypassing effortful parts of the user journey. The *inertia* lens might surface an underlying belief that the current way is the best, invoking resistance to anything new or different.

Many of the worst product and project failures we've witnessed have been based on faulty assumptions about the humans impacted. The purpose of this exercise is to get to know the human(s) you serve. It can be helpful to observe these humans 'in the wild', jotting down your observations as you go.

Design with intent

If, by some fortuitous coincidence, the target behaviours and current behaviours you've identified are perfectly aligned you can skip ahead to the next part of the framework. However, we have yet to encounter a technology solution that does not ask us to do something different, intentionally or otherwise. The key to successful product adoption lies in bridging the gap between a user's current behaviours and the target behaviours that will help them achieve their desired outcome.

For each behavioural change, we aim to address the friction that might prevent a user from reaching their desired outcome, while adding enough fuel to create momentum towards the target behaviour. The following worksheet integrates everything we've learned

Behavioural Design Worksheet

Current Behaviour(s)	Bridging the Gap				Target Behaviours

>>> Fuel >>>

Confidence	Biases	Enablers
Rewards	Social proof	Cognitive load
Self-efficacy	Reciprocity	Cognitive ease
Certainty	Likeability	Goldilocks challenges
Training	Community	MAYA Principle
Practice	Scarcity	

<<< Friction <<<

Anxieties	Biases	Constraints
Choice anxiety	Status quo bias	Resources, time
Information overload	Consistency principle	Focus
Learning anxiety	Social norms	Cognitive effort
Future anxiety	Loss aversion	Environment
	Present bias	Willpower

about humans in this book and helps to identify the forces at play. The output of this exercise will inform the ultimate design of your product.

When building these insights into product design, we essentially have two approaches to choose from:

- **Change the product** – get the product to do the heavy lifting through thoughtful design.

- **Change the person** – if you can identify a clear cue, routine and reward cycle, you can look to build new habits or disrupt old ones (refer to Chapter 11 on the role of habits).

Changing behaviours happens over time. Results are rarely immediately measurable or even apparent. Be prepared to take a long-term view of behavioural change, looking for key indicators along the way. Just like users, you will become better at behavioural design with practice. Every curious attempt is an opportunity to learn.

Deliver the change

Of course, the best-designed product in the world will not have the desired impact in an organisation, community or society unless the change is delivered successfully and users embrace and adopt the technology.

Complete the following three steps periodically to decrease disruption and increase the adoption of your technology:

1. Understand how disruptive your product or project will be using the Beckhard-Harris Change Formula detailed in Chapter 6. The change formula allows us to consider which elements of the change need to be dialled up or down to achieve a successful outcome. You can apply the formula to users, organisations or entire markets.

2. As discussed in Chapter 7, identify your stakeholders and plot them on a stakeholder matrix. This fundamental assessment of stakeholders will give you an understanding of who is impacted by your technology and who can influence its success.

3. Gain an understanding of how different stakeholders and user groups might respond to the change using the SCARF model discussed in Chapter 9. Evaluate how the change will impact their status, certainty, autonomy, relatedness and perception of fairness. This will give you an indication of whether they will move towards or away from your technology, and allow you to plan and respond accordingly.

Reflect and refine

As technologists, we need to be mindful of our own intention-action gap. Despite our best intentions, there's often a gap between the desire to act ethically and following through on ethical design. In today's world, legislation is no longer an effective guide when choosing the right thing to do. Aligning with your purpose offers an alternative lens for decision-making and guides action in the most difficult of circumstances.

As social systems become increasingly intertwined with technology, decisions taken by technologists have far-reaching consequences. The following reflection exercises will help guide decision-making along the journey:

- Refer to our framework for ethical nudging when designing product features (refer to ethical nudge framework in Chapter 20)

- Search for unintended consequences using our six-point framework (refer to Chapter 21)

- Scan for dark patterns throughout your product design (refer to popular dark patterns table in Chapter 22)

- Complete the ledger of externalities exercise (refer to Chapter 23)

These basic ethical checkpoints should be a core part of a technologist's toolkit. We envisage this process as an iterative and ever-evolving conversation between peers, stakeholders, users and other parties. We encourage you to refer to the framework periodically and particularly when making significant decisions about your product or assumptions about humans.

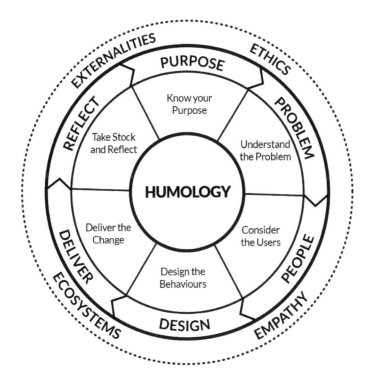

Figure 16 *Bringing it all together – the Humology framework*

Responsible technology is better technology. We wish you well on your technology journey. If you are interested in continuing your *Humology* journey, visit our website (www.Humology.com) for complementary material including case studies, chapter activities and toolkits.

Call To Action

We need your help!

Humology is not just a book or a framework. It might be an ideology, or even a philosophy. Our hope is that it becomes something more than that – a tangible representation of the movement to put humans back at the heart of technology. This book grew from our belief that technology should be created and designed with humans in mind, not just for the sake of progress. We have an opportunity to leverage technology to augment humanity and we know that you feel the same way. Not only does it make sense for us as a species, it greatly increases the chances of sustainable success with emerging technologies.

We're asking for your help to spread this message as widely as possible. And we already have some ideas:

- Host a talk at your company or university

- Share a book summary, or author a blog about human-led technology innovation

- Host or be a guest on a podcast

- Share the core message of Humology together with your thoughts with your communities and networks

No matter what avenue you take for spreading the message, we are happy to help, where possible. Let's make it happen together!

Tell us how you plan to spread the word and keep the dialogue moving. Together, we can forge a community of technologists (or humologists) that are building innovative technologies with ethical intent and compassion for humanity.

If you're interested in working with us, or if you want to get involved in this global conversation about building a better world for everyone, we would love to hear from you.

All the best,
Declan & Joanne

References

Amrine, M. (1946, June 23). *The Real Problem is in The Hearts of Man.* *New York Times* Magazine.

Angelou, M. (2018, August 12). Twitter. Available at: https://twitter.com/drmayaangelou/status/1028663286512930817?lang=en

Antliff, S. (2021, June 28). Workplace Overwhelm: How to Protect Your Team from Change Fatigue. Atlassian Work Life.

Ariely, D. (2008). *Predictably Irrational: The Hidden Forces That Shape Our Decisions.* New York: HarperCollins.

Atomi (2019, July 1). *A Level Psychology: The Cognitive Approach.* *YouTube.* Available at: www.youtube.com/watch?v=FctU-QV8ZVo

Arthur, T. S. (1848). *Advice to Young Men on Their Duties and Conduct in Life.* Boston, Mass: NC Barton.

B Lab. (nd). Available at: www.bcorporation.net/en-us

Beck, K. et al. (2001). *Manifesto for Agile Software Development.* Available at: agilemanifesto.org

Beckhard, R. and Harris, R. T. (1987). *Organizational Transitions: Managing Complex Change (2nd ed).* Reading, Mass: Addison-Wesley.

Behavioural Insights Team (nd). *Who We Are.* Available at: www.bi.team/about-us/who-we-are

Behavioral Insights Team (2017, August 15). *A Review of Optimism Bias, Planning Fallacy, Sunk Cost Bias and Groupthink in Project Delivery and Organisational Decision Making*. Available at: www.bi.team/publications/a-review-of-optimism-bias-planning-fallacy-sunk-cost-bias-and-groupthink-in-project-delivery-and-organisational-decision-making

Blaga, A. (2014, September 17). Managing Both Change and Engagement with the Commitment Curve. Available at: www.performancemagazine.org/managing-both-change-and-engagement-with-the-commitment-curve/

Boudreau, P. (2019). *Applying Artificial Intelligence to Project Management*. Canada.

Branting, H. and Lange, C. (1921). Nobel Peace Prize 1921 lecture. nobelprize.org. Available at: www.nobelprize.org/prizes/peace/1921/lange/lecture

Bruntsch, C. (2018, December 11). *Carl Rogers Client Centered Therapy*. YouTube. Available at: www.youtube.com/watch?v=UuKexVWR_7k

Budington, B. (2020, January 27). *Ring Doorbell App Packed with Third-Party Trackers*. EFF. Available at: www.eff.org/deeplinks/2020/01/ring-doorbell-app-packed-third-party-trackers

Cameron, E. and Green, M. (2015). *Making Sense of Change Management*. Kogan Page.

Carleton, R. N. (2016, June 22). Fear of the Unknown: One fear to rule them all? *Journal of Anxiety Disorders*, 41: 5–21.

Carr, N. (2011). *The Shallows: What The Internet Is Doing to our Brains*. NY: W.W. Norton.

Carroll, L. (1871). *Through the Looking-Glass*. London: Macmillan.

Cascio, J. (2020, April 29). *Facing the Age of Chaos*. Medium.com. Available at: https://medium.com/@cascio/facing-the-age-of-chaos-b00687b1f51d

Cherry, K. (2021, February 20). *What is Behaviorism? Verywell Mind*. Available at: www.verywellmind.com/behavioral-psychology-4157183

Cialdini, R. (1984). *Influence: The Psychology of Persuasion*. New York: HarperCollins.

Cialdini, R. (2016). *Pre-Suasion: A Revolutionary Way to Influence and Persuade*. New York: Simon & Schuster.

Clear, J. (2018). *Atomic Habits: An Easy & Proven Way to Build Good Habits & Break Bad Ones*. New York: Penguin Random House.

Compton, A. K. (1940). The Human Meaning of Science. *The Journal of Religion*, 20(2).

Conner, D. R. (2006). *Managing at the Speed of Change: How Resilient Managers Succeed and Prosper Where Others Fail*. New York: Random House.

Course Hero (2019, March 15). *Psychodynamic Theory | Psychology. YouTube*. Available at: www.youtube.com/watch?v=NHCok5PK-FA

Covington, T. (2021, July 30). *Distracted Driving Statistics: Research and Facts in 2021*. The Zebra. Available at: www.thezebra.com/resources/research/distracted-driving-statistics/

Cowan, N. (2001). The Magical Number 4 in Short-term Memory: A reconsideration of mental storage capacity. *Behavioral and Brain Sciences, 24(1): 87–114*.

Credit Suisse (2021). *Global Wealth Report 2021*. Available at: www.credit-suisse.com/about-us/en/reports-research/global-wealth-report.html

Csikszentmihalyi, M. (1990). *Flow: The Psychology of Optimal experience*. HarperCollins.

DiResta, R. (2018). Computational Propaganda – Public relations in a high tech age. *The Yale Review*, Vol 106(4).

Doidge, N. (2007). *The Brain That Changes Itself*. New York: Viking.

DOMO (2021, September 29). *Data Never Sleeps 9.0*. Available at: www.domo.com/learn/infographic/data-never-sleeps-9

Downes, A. (2016, January 20). *4 Learning Evaluation Models You Can Use*. eLearning Industry. Available at: https://elearningindustry.com/4-learning-evaluation-models-can-use

Dweck, C. S. (2007). *Mindset: The New Psychology of Success*. New York: Ballantine Books.

Edelman (2021,). *Edelman Trust Barometer 2021*. Available at: www.edelman.com/trust/2021-trust-barometer

Einstein, A. (1951). *'The Need for Ethical Culture'* speech on the seventy-fifth anniversary of the New York Society for Ethical Culture.

Ericsson. (2016, February). *Ericsson Mobility Report: On the pulse of the networked society*. Ericsson. Available at: http://mb.cision.com/Main/15448/2245189/661253.pdf

Eyal, N. (2014). *Hooked: How to build habit-forming products*. New York: Penguin Random House.

Fogg, B. (2020). *Tiny Habits: The Small Changes That Change Everything*. Houghton Mifflin Harcourt.

Friedman, T. L. (2016). *Thank You for Being Late: An Optimist's Guide to Thriving in the Age of Accelerations*. New York: Farrar, Straus and Giroux.

Gordon, G. (2018, September 5). *Pleasing All the People All the Time.* Praxity. Available at: www.praxity.com/insights/blogs/posts/2018/september/pleasing-all-the-people-all-the-time

Guszcza, J. (2016, January 25). *HR for Humans: How behavioral economics can reinvent HR. Deloitte.* Available at: www2.deloitte.com/us/en/insights/deloitte-review/issue-18/behavioral-economics-evidence-based-hr-management.html

Harari, Y. N. (2020, June 18). *Commencement Speech 2020: Congratulations, You are Now Hackable Animals.* Available at: www.ynharari.com/commencement-speech-2020-congratulations-you-are-now-hackable-animals

Haughey, D. (2010, January 2). *A Brief History of Project Management.* ProjectSmart. Available at: www.projectsmart.co.uk/history-of-project-management/brief-history-of-project-management.php

Hetzner, C. (2021, October 13). *Social Media's Growth-at-all-costs Mentality is Damaging Communities, Says CEO of Nextdoor.* Fortune. Available at: https://fortune.com/2021/10/13/social-media-growth-issues-nextdoor-sarah-friar

Holst, A. (2021, June 7). *Amount of Data Created, Consumed, and Stored 2010–2025.* Available at: www.statista.com/statistics/871513/worldwide-data-created

Hull, K. (2017, May 22). *Getting to the Critical Few Behaviors That Can Drive Cultural Change.* strategy+business. Available at: www.strategy-business.com/blog/Getting-to-the-Critical-Few-Behaviors-That-Can-Drive-Cultural-Change

Hunt, V., Polman, P. and Brady, D. (2021, May 6). *Stakeholder Capitalism: A conversation with Vivian Hunt and Paul Polman.* McKinsey. Available at: www.mckinsey.com/industries/public-and-social-sector/our-insights/stakeholder-capitalism-a-conversation-with-vivian-hunt-and-paul-polman

IFTF (2020). *The Hyperconnected World of 2030–2040.* Palo Alto: IFTF.org. Available at: www.iftf.org/fileadmin/user_upload/downloads/ourwork/IFTF_Hyperconnected_World_2020.pdf

Jennings, C. (2015, May 18). *70:20:10 – Beyond the Numbers.* Training Journal. Available at: www.trainingjournal.com/articles/feature/702010-%E2%80%93-beyond-numbers

Jennings, W., et al. (2021). Lack of Trust, Conspiracy Beliefs, and Social Media Use Predict COVID-19 Vaccine Hesitancy.' *Vaccines, 9*(6), 593. https://doi.org/10.3390/vaccines9060593

Jonze, S. (Director) (2013). *Her* [Motion Picture].

Kahneman, D. (2012). *Thinking, Fast and Slow*. London: Penguin.

Kellogg, K. M., Puthumana, J. S., Fong, A., Adams, K. T., Ratwani, R. M. (2021, December 1). Understanding the Types and Effects of Clinical Interruptions and Distractions Recorded in a Multihospital Patient Safety Reporting System. *Journal Patient Safety, 17*(8): e1394-e1400.

Kent, K. A. (2022, May 18). Is Attention Deficit Disorder Increasing in Adults? Wisconsin Public Radio. Available at: www.wpr. org/shows/attention-deficit-disorder-increasing-adults

Khan Academy (nd). *Humanistic Theory*. Available at: www.khanacademy.org/test-prep/mcat/behavior/theories-personality/v/humanistic-theory

Kotter, J. (2012). *Leading Change*. Boston, Massachusetts: Harvard Business School Press.

Kübler-Ross, E. (1969). *On Death and Dying*. London: Routledge.

Kuran, T. and Sunstein, C. R. (1999). Availability Cascades and Risk Regulation. *Stanford Law Review*, Vol 51(4): 683–768.

LaMorte, W. W. (2019). *Behavioral Change Models*. Boston University School of Public Health. Available at: https://sphweb.bumc. bu.edu/otlt/mph-modules/sb/behavioralchangetheories/

Landon, L. E. (1831). *Romance and Reality Vol. III*. London: Colburn & Bentley.

Lawrence, P. R. (1969). How to Deal With Resistance to Change. *Harvard Business Review*.

Lee, M. (2019, June 17). *Thrive Global and P&G Announce Groundbreaking Partnership Bringing Behavior Change to Consumers Through Microstep Habit-Stacking*. Business Wire. Available at: www.businesswire.com/news/home/20190617005150/en/Thrive-Global-and-PG-Announce-Groundbreaking-Partnership-Bringing-Behavior-Change-to-Consumers-Through-Microstep-Habit-Stacking

Leroy, S. (2009). Why is it So Hard to Do My Work? The challenge of attention residue when switching between work tasks. *Organizational Behavior and Human Decision Processes*, 109(2): 168–181. Available at: www.sciencedirect.com/science/article/abs/pii/S0749597809000399

Lewin, K. (1947). Frontiers in Group Dynamics: Concept, method and reality in social science; social equilibria and social change. *Human Relations*, 1, 5–41.

Machiavelli, N. (1532). *The Prince*. Rome: Antonio Blado d'Asola.

Masige, S. (2019). Atlassian Is Weeding out the 'Brilliant Jerks', Changing the Way It Does Performance Reviews to Reward

Workers Who Show' Heart and Balance' Not Just Technical Skills. *Business Insider Australia.*

Maslow, A. H. (1943) 'A Theory of Human Motivation'. *Psychological Review,* 50(4): 370–396.

Massey, C. (2016, February 28). *Behavioural Design – What, Why and How.* Mind the Product. Available at: www.mindtheproduct. com/behavioural-design-what-why-and-how/

McGregor, D. (1960). *The Human Side of Enterprise.* New York: McGraw-Hill.

McLeon, D. S. (2021). *Pavlov's Dogs Study and Pavlovian Conditioning Explained.* Simply Psychology. Available at: www.simply-psychology.org/pavlov.html

McLuhan, M. (1964). *Understanding Media: The Extensions of Man.* New York: McGraw-Hill.

Mertens, S., Herberz, M., Hahnel, U. J. J. and Brosch, T. (2022, January 4). The Effectiveness of Nudging: A Meta-analysis of Choice Architecture Interventions Across Behavioral Domains. *Proceedings of the National Academy of Sciences,* 119(1) e2107346118.

Microsoft Worklab. (2021, April 20). WTI Pulse Report: Research proves your brain needs breaks. Available at: https:// www.microsoft.com/en-us/worklab/work-trend-index/ brain-research

Miller, G. (1956). The Magical Number Seven Plus Or Minus Two: some limits on our capacity for processing information. *Psychological Review, 63*: 81–97.

Moore, G. A. (1991). *Crossing the Chasm: Marketing and selling technology products to mainstream customers.* New York: HarperBusiness.

Moran, M. (2003, December 10). *The Blair Witch Hunt.* NBC News Available at: www.nbcnews.com/id/wbna3070627

Morris, J., Marzano, M., Dandy, N. and O'Brien, L. (2012). *Theories and Models of Behaviour and Behaviour Change. Forest Research.* Available at: www.forestresearch.gov.uk/documents/1409/ behaviour_review_theory.pdf

Newton, I. (1687). *Philosophiæ Naturalis Principia Mathematica.* London: Halley.

Newton, J. D., *Uncommon Friends: Life with Thomas Edison, Henry Ford, Harvey Firestone, Alexis Carrel, and Charles Lindbergh.* Thomson Learning, 1987.

New York Times Events (2019, November 6). *Netflix CEO Reed Hastings Talks Streaming Wars, Apple TV+, Disney + and More*

| *DealBook*. YouTube. Available at: www.youtube.com/ watch?v=7V6FFeZdFz4

Nolsoe, E. (2021, July 16). *Is My Phone Listening to My Conversations? Britons believe the answer is yes.* YouGov. Available at: https:// yougov.co.uk/topics/technology/articles-reports/2021/ 07/16/my-phone-listening-my-conversations-britons-believ

NPR. (2021). Facebook's Parent is Being Sued by Rohingya Refugees Over Myanmar Violence. Available at: www.npr. org/2021/12/14/1064011279/facebook-is-being-sued-by-rohingya-refugees-over-myanmar-violence?t= 1647989332672

O'Donovan, K. (2020). *20 Inspiring Vision Statement Examples (2020 updated)*. Available at: www.lifehack.org/articles/ work/20-sample-vision-statement-for-the-new-startup. html

OECD (2020). *Behavioural Insights*. OECD. Available at: www.oecd. org/gov/regulatory-policy/behavioural-insights.htm

Office of Governance Commerce (2007). *Managing Successful Programmes*. London: TSO.

OGC (2009). *Managing Successful Projects with PRINCE2*. London: TSO.

Orlowski, J. (Director) (2020). *The Social Dilemma* [Motion Picture].

Panorama (2018, July 4). Smartphones: The Dark Side, series 27, episode 22, BBC. (A. Raskin, Interviewer)

Peters, T. (1987). *Thriving On Chaos: Handbook For A Management Revolution*. New York: Knopf.

Pink, D. H. (2009). *Drive: The Surprising Truth About What Motivates Us*. New York: Riverhead Books.

Pink, D. H. (2012). *To Sell is Human: The Surprising Truth About Moving Others*. New York: Riverhead Books.

PMI (nd). *What is Project Management? Project Management Institute.* Available at: www.pmi.org/about/learn-about-pmi/ what-is-project-management

Prosci (nd). *The Change Management Office (CMO)*. Prosci. Available at: www.prosci.com/resources/articles/change-management-office-primer

Reagan, G. (2009, July 13). *The Evolution of Facebook's Mission Statement. Observer.* Available at: https://observer.com/ 2009/07/the-evolution-of-facebooks-mission-statement

RingCentral. (2019). From Workplace Chaos to Zen. Available at: https://netstorage.ringcentral.com/documents/connected_ workplace.pdf

Rock, D. (2008). SCARF: A Brain-based Model for Collaborating With and Influencing Others. *NeuroLeadership Journal*.

Satir, V., Banmen, J. and Gomori, M. (1991). *The Satir Model: Family Therapy and Beyond*. Palo Alto, California: Science and Behavior Books.

Scheiber, N. (2017) How Uber Uses Psychological Tricks to Push its Drivers' Buttons. *The New York Times*. [Online]. Available at: www.nytimes.com/interactive/2017/04/02/technology/uber-drivers-psychological-tricks.html.

Schein, E.H. (1996). Kurt Lewin's Change Theory in the Field and in the Classroom: Notes toward a model of managed learning. *Systems Practice*, 9, 27–47.

Schopenhauer, A. (1851). 'On Noise' from *Essays of A. Schopenhauer*. New York.

Seymour, T., & Hussein, S. (2014). The History of Project Management. *International Journal of Management and Information Systems*.

Shakespeare, W., (1622) *Othello*. London: Clarendon Press.

Shaw, G. B. (1903). *Man and Superman*. London: A. Constable.

Simply Wall St. (2021, November 15). Investors One-year Losses Grow to 34% as the Stock Sheds US$52m this Past Week. Nasdaq.com. Available at: www.nasdaq.com/articles/investors-one-year-losses-grow-to-34-as-the-stock-sheds-us%2452m-this-past-week-2021-11-15

Sinek, S. (2009). *Start with Why: How Great Leaders Inspire Everyone to Take Action*. London: Portfolio/Penguin.

Smiles, S. (1856). *Character: The true gentleman*.

Sparrow, B., Liu, J., and Wegner, D. M. (2011). Google Effects on Memory: Cognitive consequences of having information at our fingertips. *Science*, 333, 776–778.

Sunstein, C. R. (2021). *Sludge: What Stops Us from Getting Things Done and What to Do about It*. Cambridge, Massachusetts: The MIT Press.

Sweller, J. A. (2011). *Cognitive Load Theory*. New York: Springer.

Sydow, L. (2021, January 28). *Health Fitness Downloads Rose 30 Percent*. App Annie. Available at: www.appannie.com/en/insights/market-data/health-fitness-downloads-rose-30-percent/

Tesla, N. (1910). What Science May Achieve this Year. *What Science May Achieve This Year*, 1910. Available at: https://teslauniverse.com/nikola-tesla/articles/what-science-may-achieve-year

Tessian (2022). *25 Biggest GDPR Fines So Far (2019, 2020, 2021, 2022)*. Available at: www.tessian.com/blog/biggest-gdpr-fines-2020/

Thaler, R. H. and Sunstein, C. R. (2008). *Nudge: Improving Decisions About Health, Wealth and Happiness*. Caravan Books.

Thompson, D. (2017). *Hit Makers: The science of popularity in an age of distraction*. New York: Penguin.

Thoreau, H. D. (1854). *Where I Lived, and What I Lived For*. Walden.

Ulwick, A. (2016). *Jobs to be Done: Theory to Practice*. Houston: Idea Bite Press.

United Nations (2021). *UN Behavioural Science Report*. Available at: www.uninnovation.network/assets/BeSci/UN_Behavioural_Science_Report_2021.pdf

Voltaire. (1785). *Oeuvres Completes, Volume 46*.

Washington, G. (1780, 5 March). Letter to Lord Stirling.

Watson, A. (2021, November 26). *Social Media as a News Source Worldwide 2021*. Statista. Available at: www.statista.com/statistics/718019/social-media-news-source/

Weinberg, G. M. (1992). *Quality Software Management V1 – Systems Thinking*. New York: Dorset House Publishing

Westwood, J. (2021, June 23). *Cristiano Ronaldo Coca-Cola controversy: Euro 2020 press conference incident explained*. Goal.com. Available at: www.goal.com/en-ie/news/cristiano-ronaldo-coca-cola-controversy-euro-2020-press/boc10jxcu1791950qedw9ydzf

Whitehead, A.N. (1911). *An Introduction to Mathematics*. Williams & Northgate.

Wylie, C. (2019). *Mindf*ck: Inside Cambridge Analytica's Plot*. London: Profile Books.

Yeykelis,L., Cummings, J. J. and Reeves, B. (2014, January 7). Multitasking on a Single Device: Arousal and the Frequency, Anticipation, and Prediction of Switching Between Media Content on a Computer. *Journal of Communication*, 64(1): 167–192.

Youyou, W., Kosinski, M. and Stillwell, D. (2015). Computers Judge Personalities Better than Humans. *Proceedings of the National Academy of Sciences*, 112(4): 1036–1040.

Zaltman, G. (2003). *How Customers Think*. Boston: Harvard Business Press.

The Authors

Declan Foster is an industry leader in change management and project delivery, and provides consulting services to clients globally and is ranked in the top 25 Thought Leaders in project management. He worked in consulting and HR Tech in London before moving to Australia, where he spent several years working as a management consultant for PwC Consulting. In 2005, he became an independent consultant providing change management and project delivery expertise. He is always keen to learn about different industries, and he has worked in diverse organisations, including banks, not-for-profits, public transport and airlines.

Declan recently returned to his hometown of Dublin, where he occasionally admits to missing the Australian sunshine. He is the founder of Martello Change Consulting, providing change management and project delivery services to clients globally. He has written articles for leading technology websites and is a regular and active contributor on LinkedIn.

Declan believes in lifelong learning and has recently studied Behavioural Economics and received an honours degree in Artificial Intelligence.

Joanne Griffin is a strategist, innovator and transformation professional with a lengthy career in finance and technology. Her career spans more than 25 years across various industries, including senior leadership positions at LinkedIn, Nielsen and EY. She is currently CEO at AdaptIQ where she leads innovative initiatives focused on transformation and adaptability for global enterprises. A solutions-builder at heart with a deep appreciation of the power of community to solve complex challenges, she is co-founder and COO of IrelandTogether.ie, a non-profit organisation creating opportunity for entrepreneurs by creating serendipitous collisions.

Her enduring love affair with technology dates back to the arrival of the Commodore VIC-20 in the early 1980s. She believes that technologists have a responsibility to be ethical, collaborative and transparent in the design of products and business models. She advises a small number of high-potential start-ups who are aligned with those values.

Joanne has an impressive record of contributions to curriculums, research bodies and publications in the field of technology. She also serves as a judge for technology awards and competitions globally.

⊕ www.Humology.com

Lightning Source UK Ltd.
Milton Keynes UK
UKHW020615290722
406557UK00005B/104